© Copyright 2024 by TERENCE LAMBERT - All rights reserved.

The following Book is reproduced below with the goal of providing information that is as accurate and reliable as possible. Regardless, purchasing this Book can be seen as consent to the fact that both the publisher and the author of this book are in no way experts on the topics discussed within and that any recommendations or suggestions that are made herein are for entertainment purposes only. Professionals should be consulted as needed prior to undertaking any of the action endorsed herein.

This declaration is deemed fair and valid by both the American Bar Association and the Committee of Publishers Association and is legally binding throughout the United States. Furthermore, the transmission, duplication, or reproduction of any of the following work including specific information will be considered an illegal act irrespective of if it is done electronically or in print. This extends to creating a secondary or tertiary copy of the work or a recorded copy and is only allowed with the express written consent from the Publisher. All additional right reserved.

The information in the following pages is broadly considered a truthful and accurate account of facts and as such, any inattention, use, or misuse of the information in question by the reader will render any resulting actions solely under their purview. There are no scenarios in which the publisher or the original author of this work can be in any fashion deemed liable for any hardship or damages that may befall them after undertaking information described herein.

Additionally, the information in the following pages is intended only for informational purposes and should thus be thought of as universal. As befitting its nature, it is presented without assurance regarding its prolonged validity or interim quality. Trademarks that are mentioned are done without written consent and can in no way be considered an endorsement from the trademark holder.

Table of Contents

Introduction — 8
Chapter 1: Why Choose a Container Home? — 11
The Benefits of Shipping Container Homes — 12
Accessibility — 12
Time-Saving — 12
Affordable To Build — 13
Friendly for the Setting (Green Living) — 13
Weather-Proof — 13
Excellent Flexibility — 14
Shipping Container Homes Solving the Problems of Home Building — 14

Chapter 2: Things to Consider Before the Whole Construction Process — 17
Go See an Actual Shipping Container — 18
Determine The Budget — 18
Do a Physical Survey of the Building Site? — 19
Decide On the Exact Project Requirements — 19
Create a Layout and Floor Plan — 19
Finalize The Design — 19

Chapter 3: Choosing a Shipping Container — 21
Price Of Containers — 22
Size of the Container — 23
Type of the Container — 23
Condition of the Container — 24
Damage You Should Look Out For — 24
Rear Header — 24
Crash Rail — 24
Rear Top Plate — 24
Hinge — 24
Lock Rod — 25
Hinge Guard — 25
Rear Post — 25
Custom Catches/ Seal — 25
Cam And Keeper — 25
Door Handle — 25

Rear Sill	25
Door Panel	25
Bearing Bracket	25
Floor	26
Bottom Side Rail	26
Forklift Pocket	26
Front Sill	26
Front Panel	26
Front Corner Post	26
Corner Casting	27
Front Top Rail	27
Front Header	27
Roof	27
Top Side Rail	27
Chapter 4: Plans	**28**
Plan 1	29
Plan 2	31
Plan 3	35
Plan 4	37
Plan 5	39
Plan 6	41
Plan 7	43
Plan 8	45
Plan 9	47
Plan 10	49
Chapter 5: Permits and Zoning Laws	**51**
Australia	52
New Zealand	52
United Kingdom	52
United States	52
General List of Documents Required	53
Chapter 6: Steps in Building Your Container Home	**54**
Site Works	55
Foundation	55
Modifications to the Container	55
Setting and Securing the Containers to the Foundation	56
Adding A Roof	56

Installing Architectural Elements	56
Installing Utilities, Fixtures and Floors	56
Sign-Off and Inspection	57

Chapter 7: Buying a Shipping Container — 58

New Or Used?	59
Rust	59
Leaks	59
Chemical Contamination	60
Functional Doors and Locks	60
Wooden Flooring in Good Repair	60
Intact Identification Code	60
Where Can I Get One?	61
What's the Price by Size?	61
Container Purchasing Checklist	62

Chapter 8: Preparing the Land — 63

Foundations	64
Concrete Piers	64
Slab-On-Grade	64
Pile Foundation	65
Strip Foundation	65
Concrete	65
Footings	67
Fixing The Container	69

Chapter 9: Should You Do It or Let the Professionals? — 70

Tips for Finding an Experienced Contractor	71
Feel Comfortable with Your Decision	72
About Contractor Bonds	73

Chapter 10: Insulation — 75

Cork Insulation	76
Spray Foam	76
Wool Insulation	77
Cotton Insulation	77
Fiberglass	77
Cellulose	78
Factors Affecting Choice of Insulation	78
Types Of Insulation	79
Wall and Ceiling Insulation Application	79

External Insulation — 80
Internal Insulation — 80

Chapter 11: Utilities — 82
Electricity — 83
Gas — 84
Sewer And Septic — 84
Telecommunications — 85
Water — 85

Chapter 12: Installation of Doors and Windows — 86
Installation Requirements — 87
Planning for Windows and Doorways — 88
Can I Put in a Sliding Glass Door? — 88
Doorways — 89
Rollup Door — 89
Traditional Residential Door — 89
Let's Talk Windows — 90
Can I Put a Skylight in My Container? — 91

Chapter 13: Designing Your Home — 93
Exterior Design Ideas — 94
Interior Design Ideas and Modifications — 95

Chapter 14: Success Stories — 97
Solution to Housing Problems — 98
Containers Of Hope — 99
Social Housing — 100
Six Oaks — 100
The 12 Container House — 101

Chapter 15: Frequently Asked Questions — 103
Is There a Chance of Getting Baked Inside a Shipping Container Home in Hot Weathers? — 104
In Which States Can I Build Shipping Container Homes? — 104
Will My Shipping Container Home Rust and Corrode? — 104
Will My Shipping Container Home Hold Any Value? — 105
Is Any Permit Required for Building a Shipping Container Home? — 105
Are Container Homes Sustainable? — 105
Can Shipping Container Homes Turn Out to Be Toxic? — 106
Do I Need to Get a Foundation for My Shipping Container Home? — 106
Is Shipping Container Home a Bad Choice? — 106

Chapter 16: Sustainable Living with Your Shipping Container Homes — 108
Appliances — 109
Use Sustainable Resources — 110
Recycle — 110
Grow Food — 110
Build Local — 111

Conclusion — 112
References — 116

INTRODUCTION

In this busy world, we live in today, the land that is available for real estate is quickly diminishing as the population keeps increasing across the globe. Overpopulation is causing living conditions to become difficult for many and overcrowding is becoming more of a concern with each passing day. The more people we have in our world; the fewer places we are going to have available to live in. The prices of houses are skyrocketing to the point that many cannot afford to buy them or even rent them. Many people are living on the streets of major cities because they are unable to afford rent.

More people today are beginning to realize that we need to think more seriously about living with less. Many people in the world today practice living a minimalist lifestyle. Tiny houses are becoming very popular, making the lives of many much simpler. The number of people that are actually downsizing is really quite small when compared to the current world problems we are facing today. People are becoming more interested in the container home niche.

The idea of using shipping containers as homes is not by any means a new one, as the military has been using them for a long time. This has caught on to the point where more of the general public are seeking their own container homes. The niche is not a standardized one yet so there are still areas within it that need to be improved. There are only a few professionals that can claim to know how to operate the container vans properly. Some people decided to construct their own homes and have come up with some impressive results.

Here are some testimonies from people who have already lived in container houses:

"I have been living in a shipping container for almost a year now and I've fallen in love with it. It is everything that I hoped it would be. The advantages are several: First, there is plenty of room to stand, walk, sit and sleep. Second, the container offers great protection from pests and other insects. It's very comfortable to be in. Third, when you go to use the bathroom, you have the opportunity to stand up straight instead of bending over a hole in the floor! Fourth, you don't have a draft outside your home because everything is insulated well."

- David Henshaw

"I live in a 40-foot shipping container and I love it! I occasionally get the urge to ask my neighbors what they think about this, but so far, they haven't complained, so I'm glad. One reason to build a shipping container home is the cost. Most materials for a home are still more expensive than buying a shipping container. Shipping containers are very portable. They can be moved with a truck, car, or even boat trailer. The cost of land might make them not an economically feasible option for some people, but moving them makes the housing available to more people."

· Kim Bayss

"We have been living in our shipping container now for nearly three years and it has worked out great. The place we built is about the size of a small house and we have managed to make it very comfortable. The insulation is great and we don't feel any drafts in the winters. We like the way it looks and we like living in a home that feels and looks more like a real house instead of an RV. If you are on the fence about this idea, then I suggest that you do some research into shipping container homes before dismissing it."

· Tommy M.

These are just some of the testimonies from people who have lived in these types of houses.

I hope to accomplish helping you do this through the information in this book. Let us now move into the world of containers and get to know what they are really all about so you will be able to make a shipping container home that you will be proud of!

To make sure that you are not going to make bad choices that could end up being disastrous for you, I have some tips and suggestions within these pages that I hope will offer you secure guidelines that you can follow when making decisions regarding the building of your shipping container home. To avoid bad situations while working on a project, it will certainly be worth your while to read this book. You have certainly taken a step in the right direction to help ensure that you are off to a good start with the building of your shipping container home just by downloading this book.

CHAPTER 1
Why Choose a Container Home?

The Benefits of Shipping Container Homes

You will appreciate these advantages first-hand and see them for yourself if you are lucky enough to have created your own and/or live in one.

When it comes to building your own home, used containers are versatile, sturdy, modular-friendly and just an all-around winner, much cheaper than traditional construction techniques for timber-framed houses and brick and mortar structures.

It is now possible to use shipping containers for other purposes. These containers are now one of the best choices, considering the limited space and growing costs of building houses or offices. There were rumors that a branch of Starbucks was only made up of two containers. Looking at the interior design of the container, it looked like an elegant place to rest.

This makes them ideal for architectural homes as well. They deliver minimal costs for building material and can be easily changed. With two containers, you'll already have a nice location. While there were earlier prefabricated buildings, they were never intended as a place to conduct business.

Accessibility

The best price tag for building materials vs. steel containers will be the latter. You face financial difficulties each time you build a house; this will minimize the house's cost in so many ways.

Time-Saving

It takes time to construct a traditional building. From the moment the base is built to the end of the concrete supporting beams, there is no house or office. Prefabricated structures such as containers can easily become a functional office if you quickly need office space. This saves lag in the house-building process. The building of a metal container can quickly become an elegant room.

The average time to prepare and transport a shipping container is in the range of two months. This involves the time from the initial purchase to the complete personalization to create a comfortable home or office environment.

Furthermore, many companies are specializing in fitting containers for the fastest performance. It is nevertheless possible for those who want a more hands-on approach to fully complete the fit when the container is shipped and located.

Affordable To Build

The average cost of this sort of home or office is very affordable. It is cheaper to purchase a container and turn it into a secure and comfortable home than to buy a normal property in a cheap area of town.

A used container can currently be picked up for about $1,500USD. This is the base cost for 305sq feet of floor space. When you compare it to the expense of more conventional building forms, it's a pretty good deal.

Used container homes are more economical to produce than traditional methods of construction.

Friendly for the Setting (Green Living)

So how green can vibrant shipping containers be?

Response: They can be as green as you would like them to be.

Think of your home more like an "eco-pod" if you want to go down a very green path. By placing a few solar panels on the roof, you could generate your electricity. If you're close to a river or a quick-flowing stream, you can use hydro.

A "Green/Living Roof" can be added to the top of your containers to help separate and drastically reduce heating and cooling costs in the winter (in the summer).

Weather-Proof

Consider the fact that shipping containers on hundreds of thousands of miles of open-top trans-oceanic shipping container vessels are designed to endure the most unforgiving environmental conditions and constructed before being decommissioned to have a minimum work life of 20 years. After that, these containers have an almost endless lifespan, in a fixed location.

They are made from pre-fabricated steel and welded, making them strong and rigid, and very durable. This makes them especially well-suited for high geologic activity areas, such as hurricane hotspots and earthquake zones.

Shipping containers can keep up to 175mp/h (281km/h) safely against wind speeds when anchored to pylons, which is easy to do. Whether it is constructed from used shipping containers or a conventional building, each building should have adequate foundations.

I listed the three main advantages above that most homeowners would note immediately.

In truth, they are the three key things many people look at when buying any kind of home. It also reveals that the boom in shipping container homes has been entirely justifiable in the last few years and why so many individuals turn to these containers to create their own dream homes.

With the right internal floor plans, a comfortable and practical space can be created, with everything you need to relax in style.

Although it can sound like there are many difficulties in turning a container into a home, the whole process is usually straightforward. Once the secondary container has been purchased and shipped to your territory, it is simply a process of acquiring the correct plans for the intended purpose. The professionals will benefit from a high-quality finish. Moreover, experts would certainly need to install windows, doors, power supplies and the like.

Excellent Flexibility

If the container has been purchased, the internal configuration and most essential features can be customized. It typically helps to look at various floor plans and floor sizes to understand what is available and create the layout to meet your particular needs. The traditional 20-foot container is an excellent way to turn it into a house since it is simpler to navigate and is better suited for combining it with other units.

The 40-foot model is a choice for those looking for more interior space and provides access to almost 300 square ft. of space. Also, the wider container provides more versatility in separating internal space into different spaces.

Shipping Container Homes Solving the Problems of Home Building

It's the pinnacle of one's accomplishments to own a house. It is out of reach for most people, however, with growing homeownership costs. Owing to rapidly rising costs, land scarcity and environmental issues, many are looking at alternatives to the conventional brick and mortar residences that we all know.

One of the main advantages of using a container for shipping is that it already has walls, floors and a roof! You can attempt to incorporate many containers into a single dwelling with the aid of architects and designers. By proper planning and design, windows, doors and fascias are incorporated to make the finished product look more comparable to a typical home.

Shipping containers are very robust—they are usually made from corrugated steel weathering. To ensure you stay cool during hot weather and don't freeze to death during the winter, you'll need to look into keeping this properly insulated!

Don't be tricked into expecting shabby interiors—oh no! It is possible to completely outfit shipping container homes with beautiful interiors with modern designs, resulting in a stunning finish. The basics of modern plumbing and electrical appliances are also included, of course.

Although you can design projects of this kind yourself (with some necessary help), there are now many companies that provide turnkey home building services with completely designed and pre-built container homes that can be delivered and installed on your building plot.

The speed of construction is one of the main advantages of this approach—the advantages of a modular approach (joining shipping cans together) is that the construction time is quick—so fast, it is usually completed in a fraction of the time it would take a conventional home construction.

There are some parallels with a traditional home building—usually, you'll need foundations to be laid—you'll need utilities for plumbing and electricity. There could be local building codes that you will have to comply with, and your new home will require funding, as is the case with most things.

Shipping container homes are an answer to many homes building issues. They offer an environmentally friendly approach to reusing existing materials for a surprising alternative function!

It is thrilling to think that the overseas shipping container that carried your TV is now going to be the home you live in. In the early 1950s, families in America could buy a modest new home for around $20,000 after you added property taxes, furniture, appliances and moving-in expenses.

In today's real estate market, buying the same type of house in a typical middle-class neighborhood could cost you around $200,000, depending on the location and other factors.

But now, as their parents or grandparents did for around $20,000 in the 1950s, many people are buying their new homes for the same amount. The difference is that homes that are not made of wood or traditional materials are bought.

For homes, they purchase shipping containers. Designed from recycled steel containers that once carried goods on large ships, these are right-homes and, at first, they're not what you might think. There are spacious homes which are appealing.

Many people are studying the use of recycled shipping containers as a source of material for constructing homes. They are a green alternative to other items and using them does a lot of good for the recycling community.

We don't think too much about it, but there are plenty of unused, empty shipping containers sitting at ports worldwide, taking up space and doing nothing, or even worse, being sent off to the landfill.

Goods manufacturers and shipping companies that sell these items see them as cheap goods, throwaways like soda cans because they don't see the value for many consumers. Shipping unused and empty containers back to their country of origin is very expensive for countries. When the need for them arises, purchasing new containers is most often cheaper.

Costs for shipping containers vary, but for around $1,500 on average, you can get a used one. The average container has 350 square feet of space. Anyone who wants a 3,000 square foot home would have to spend about $80 per square foot to get a house built using traditional techniques.

Container homes cost around $4 and a half per container per square foot (the frame's cost, which is not included in the construction and finishing work). It's still quite a savings over traditional home building techniques, even with the added cost of installing and finishing the basic units to transform them into a home.

The most common areas for building cargo container houses have been parts of Asia and the former Soviet Union. But shipping container homes have recently begun to show up in the United States, particularly in southern California.

Of course, repairing these steel containers requires construction work, including installing insulation, plumbing, electricity, windows and doors. But homes are built of recycled materials, inexpensive and distinctive; after all, right now, this is just what awaits many green homeowners.

CHAPTER 2
Things to Consider Before the Whole Construction Process

Planning is the real key to a build that is efficient, economical and achievable. Even before coming up with a design plan, there are many factors that need to be considered. Proper preparation ensures that the build goes smoothly when it is actually underway.

All in all, this will result in a complete profile of the project: the scope, the budget and the risks and difficulties to be potentially experienced during the build.

That said, figuring out where to begin can be daunting, especially for a first construction project. Following a checklist (like the one shown here) can be a great way to get started.

Go See an Actual Shipping Container

Obviously, shipping containers are needed to build a shipping container home. That is why the first step is to find an actual container and give it a thorough examination. Get a concrete idea of what the space really looks like. This will help in figuring out the overall design later and in keeping expectations in the realm of the feasible.

This is also a chance to compare the quality and price of containers from different sources, should there be more than one in an area. When surveying used containers, keep an eye out for ones that have minimal damage.

Determine The Budget

It's easy to just name a price and call it the budget, but really, that's not how things should be done.

Coming up with a budget requires a look at every aspect of the build. Get an idea of the construction, labor and professional fees. Minimize the risk of incurring unexpected expenses by being as thorough as possible.

Consulting architects and contractors is a great way to get a more concrete idea of how much a project will cost. It is also advisable to get in contact with companies who sell containers and do modifications.

It is best to keep the budget a little below the amount of money that is actually available. This margin will cover any unanticipated expenses that are to be expected during any construction project.

Do a Physical Survey of the Building Site?

The choice of the building site is crucial. One big factor to consider is the soil bearing capacity—referring to the capacity of the soil to support the structural load applied to the ground.

The location of a house will also determine the ease of access and the degree of privacy. Try to see how far the site is from the road or highway. Will it be necessary to add an extended driveway? Concerns like this can increase the cost of the build and should be taken into account during budgeting.

Decide On the Exact Project Requirements

Get started on a "wish list." In particular, focus on the number of rooms that are needed. Decide on how many bedrooms and bathrooms there will be, and on whether rooms will be constructed for utilities like the kitchen and dining area. Detail any additional features desired, such as a home office space, a game room, or the like. Make an estimate of the rough square footage required for each, and for the whole project.

However, prepare to negotiate. Most likely, adjustments will need to be made in coming up with the final design or during the course of the build. Try your best to be flexible and to be open to new ideas and suggestions from professionals.

Create a Layout and Floor Plan

Once the "wish list" is ready, start sketching a layout and floor plan for the home. Make sure to draw the dimensions to scale. This will give a better idea of what the finished product will actually look like after completion.

Remember to incorporate all the functional elements that should be in the home, outlining the correct number of rooms and their purpose. Incorporate as many ideas as possible, but don't overcrowd the space. The key to a comfortable living area is a balanced utilization of space. Even a room with a small area can feel relatively expansive with a successful interior layout.

Finalize The Design

A general idea is all well and good, but once that's done, it's time to get into the specifics. There are a few ways to go about designing a shipping container home.

One is to hire an architect to come up with the design based on the outlined specifications. This has the advantage of producing a completely unique and original home that will cater to specific needs or preferences.

However, there is a downside. Since shipping container homes are still relatively rare, it may be a challenge to find someone who is willing and able to design the home. There are many design considerations unique to shipping container homes that the average architect—no matter how skilled—may be unfamiliar with.

An alternative is to locate a design entity that offers turnkey home designs. "Turnkey" means the design is ready to use once purchased. The source company will offer several "stock" designs to choose from. These ready-made "kit" designs can then be adapted to the building site.

Although this doesn't allow for extensive customization, it has the advantage of taking less time and costing less overall. Should there be non-negotiable aspects of the home, which should absolutely be included in the design, look for a company that is willing to customize, although this will probably increase the cost.

Additionally, having the final design is essential in coming up with the final budget. These plans and drawings, among other documents, are also needed in applying for building permits and getting authorization for construction.

CHAPTER 3
Choosing a Shipping Container

Choosing a container to use as a home or office isn't as easy as some people would think. Perhaps the easiest part is to go down to the shipyard where all the containers are stacked up and paying for it. That's basically it.

Most of the information you glean off the internet or from books is the choosing part. Why do most people leave out this very important detail? Well, basically because it is a very boring, tedious and time-consuming task that doesn't pique anyone's interest at all.

But, if you're planning on getting a container to turn it into a home or an office, you need to deal with this very specific detail. You need to pay attention to everything concerning the container before you even reach into your pocket to pay for it.

So, let's start with some of the key things you need to look out for: The Price and the condition or state that the container is in when you see it. These two can fluctuate greatly based on your assessment and negotiation with the shipyard manager.

Subsequently, the worse the shape the container is in, the lower the price you can get it for. Some people may scoff at this as the general mentality towards buying anything is to get the highest quality at the best price. This can be a little bit more flexible for containers especially if your plans fit the current condition, it's in for the price you can agree on.

If, for example, you're going to cut out huge chunks of the container, there's little to no sense of buying one that's in pristine condition. Although it basically means that there's going to be little to no repair work done to it after cutting huge portions of your container—that's not just cost-effective as you're led to think.

Moving on, let's talk about the price:

Price Of Containers

The going price for a container in pristine condition also depends on the size of the container. This also depends highly on the location of the shipyard and its distance from the construction site. These are things you have to pay attention to as they can really affect the price of the container. As for the basic price of the container, a 40-footer can cost you anywhere from around $1400 to $1600. Everything else after that, like transportation and the rental of a crane, is entirely up to you.

Size of the Container

When you start planning to create a container home or office, you're going to encounter the consideration of size. For example, you can't have a 40-footer in a small lot nor would it be practical to have a very small container to serve as a full-time home. Simply put, the size of your container is very crucial to your plans and the realization of the project.

Type of the Container

By now everybody already knows what a container basically looks like. What not everyone knows is that there are actually a lot of different types of containers. For example: what everyone already knows about containers is that there is the 20-foot and 40-foot variety. But then there's an even bigger, as well as smaller, container that is also available for people to use in their designs. There are 45 footers and 10 footers out there that you could incorporate into your design.

Here are the types of containers and what you could possibly do with them:

- Standard containers—these are the containers you regularly see as container structures like container homes or offices.
- Hi-Cube containers—these are fantastic as the high ceiling space adds more roominess to the entire structure. These are also the second most popular type of containers (regardless of size) made into container structures.
- Open top containers—open top containers have tarpaulins instead of metal roofs to cover them. These can be used just like a standard container but instead of having the metal roof you can devise one out of any material you so choose. This is perfect for those who are planning to have high roofs not necessarily made of metal.
- Open containers—these containers basically just comprise 4 solid posts. These can be used as connecting rooms to other containers and can either be boarded up to remove the exposed areas or left as is to have an open-air space in between 2 or more containers without deviating from the basic plan of having a container structure.

Condition of the Container

Containers are essentially complete by themselves and can be used immediately as a home or office with little to no modifications done to it. Now, based on your plan, you have to look at the condition of the container to ascertain if this is the one you need for your container structure. Ideally, one in pristine condition is the container to go for but if you're going to cut large portions out of it, you might as well look for containers that have some damage in the parts you intend to cut off.

For example: if you're going to cut out a huge section of the sidewall to connect it with another container, just look for a container that has major damage in that area. Not only is this a very cost-efficient way to go (damaged containers sell for less than that with little to no damage at all) but it will also make your work faster as the damaged sections are already compromised and can easily be removed with minimal effort.

Assess your plan and buy accordingly.

Damage You Should Look Out For

A container is made up of several parts. Each one of these parts sustains some form of damage in varying degrees over time. Therefore, it is in your best interest to check each part to make sure you're getting the right container in the best condition possible for your project.

Rear Header

This component can easily be dented or dinged through the active use of the container. This can be damaged from colliding with other containers and massive damage should automatically disqualify the purchase of the container.

Crash Rail

This can be damaged through dents and dings and can easily be replaced or repaired.

Rear Top Plate

This can be damaged through dents and dings and can easily be replaced or repaired.

Hinge

This can be damaged through dents and dings and can easily be replaced or repaired.

Lock Rod

This can be damaged through dents and dings and can easily be replaced or repaired.

Hinge Guard

This can be damaged through dents and dings and can easily be replaced or repaired.

Rear Post

This is an extremely hard component of the container and damage to this portion should disqualify the purchase of the container.

Custom Catches/ Seal

This is basically an aesthetic portion of your container and will also incur the same amount of damage if it has seen a lot of work transporting items at sea. You can remove this entirely or leave it as is to keep up with the image that this is a container home or office.

Cam And Keeper

Massive damage to this component should automatically disqualify the purchase unless you have a replacement ready and at no extra cost.

Door Handle

This can be damaged through dents and dings and can easily be replaced or repaired.

Rear Sill

This can be damaged through dents and dings and can easily be replaced or repaired.

Door Panel

This can be damaged through dents and dings and can easily be replaced or repaired.

Bearing Bracket

Massive damage to this component should automatically disqualify the purchase unless you have a replacement ready and at no extra cost.

Floor

The floors inside a container incur just as much damage as its exterior. This is where the cargo comes in and is prone to scratching, dents, dings, and even breaking. Luckily, most floors are wood laid on top of the metal floor, so this means you can partially replace a section of the floor or remove it entirely and replace it with a new one entirely. This is a better option as the replacement of the entire roof will open up a lot of possibilities with your floor choice and arrangement.

Furthermore, spillage can happen to the floors which would necessitate a general clean-up to ensure no harmful chemicals reside inside the container.

Bottom Side Rail

These are easily dented through transfers from the shipyard to the construction site. That's not to mention that the side rail can be bent if the container is accidentally dropped from a certain height onto another container or a hard surface. This should disqualify the purchase if extensive damage is seen.

Forklift Pocket

These are essential components of your container as these forklift pockets help in transporting the container from one place to another. Damage from forklifts can't be avoided and these pockets often show a lot of wear and tear, luckily these can easily be repaired and once back to 100 percent, they're fully serviceable. Look for broken straps or warped pockets and assess if it is within your capability and budget to repair them.

Front Sill

These often incur bumps, dents and dings and can easily be repaired through basic metalwork.

Front Panel

These often incur bumps, dents and dings and can easily be repaired through basic metalwork.

Front Corner Post

These often get damaged from bumping into other containers and are going to show lots of dings and dents. Essentially, this is one of the strongest parts of your container and a heavily damaged one should automatically disqualify the purchase of such a container.

Corner Casting

These are the hardest parts of the container and essentially the strongest. Damage to these parts should automatically disqualify the purchase of the container (unless you already planned for this) as the structure is compromised beyond repair. Replacement of the corner castings can be done but this is a very costly operation and the purchase of another container is a much better option. For containers with this type of damage, it is better to use them for replacement parts as long as there is still a chance that you can salvage the majority of the container.

Front Top Rail

Front top rails are vulnerable to bending if large weights are dropped directly on them. These can also warp over time through excessive heat or rust and corrosion brought about by the combination of salty air and water.

Front Header

These can warp over time and can easily be remedied through part replacement.

Roof

One of the most vulnerable points on a container is its roof. It is just not strong enough to support any weight. Heavy loads resting on top of containers for long periods can eventually weigh it down, moving it further away from the posts. Furthermore, rust in these areas can compromise the strength of the roof and accelerate damage caused by heavy burdens resting on top of these roofs.

Top Side Rail

The top side rail can bend if the container was handled incorrectly or a large weight (like accidentally dropping another container on it) fell directly on top of the top side rails. These can be remedied by replacing the entire top side rail or incrementally

CHAPTER 4
Plans

Plan 1

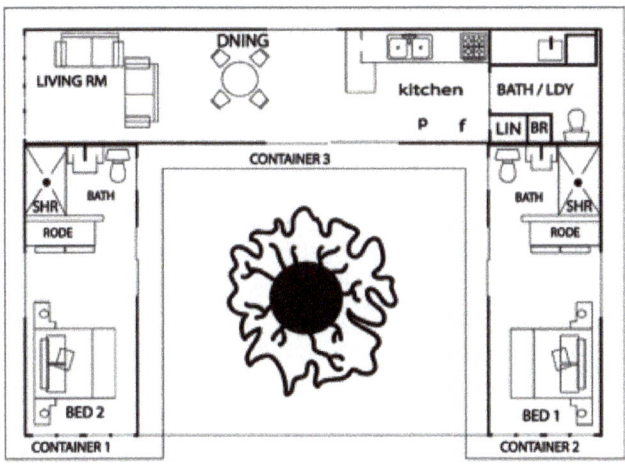

As you can see, this is a three-container architectural plan for a beautiful home with a wide area. The square footage of this home will depend on the sizes of the containers (20 ft. versus 40 ft.), but this one is spacious enough for a small family. That this home is made out of three shipping containers made it possible to include not one, but two living rooms and—even two bathrooms. There is also room for dedicated furniture like a dining table. The best part is you also have a wide deck area that complements the entire house.

You can bring in some outdoor furniture and make your deck area the perfect setting for a spring or fall evening. It is also ideal for barbecues and any gatherings you would like in your shipping container home.

Plan 2

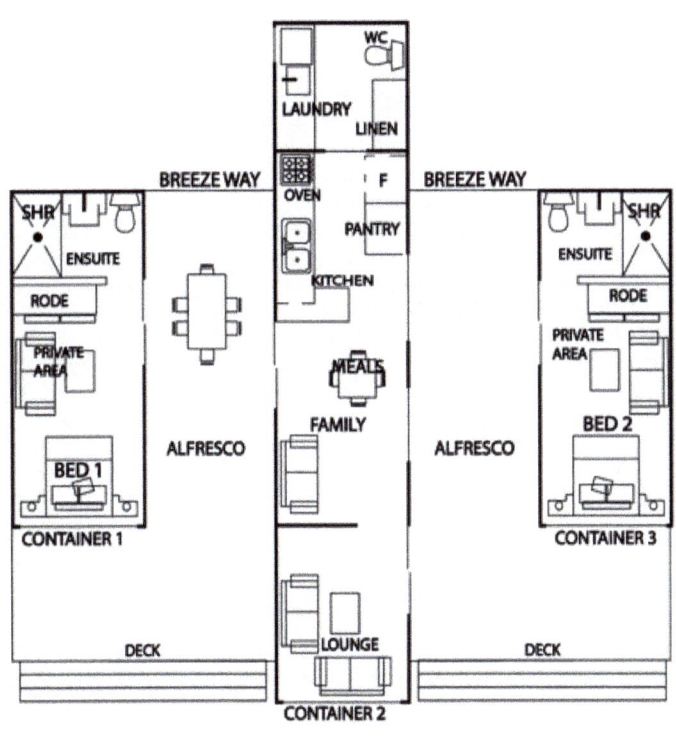

This is another excellent example of a three-container home, though you might notice a difference in the size. This displays an important fact: there is no rule that says that you should buy all the same-sized containers for your home. You could buy a 20 ft. one and a 40 ft. one. Or you could buy two 20 ft. containers and a third 40 ft., similar to this plan. And you can obviously get them the same sizes. The choice is yours, and you can play around with the design as you please, like in this incredible shipping container home.

This home's design puts a lot of emphasis on outdoor spaces, as evidenced in the plans. There's a lot of open space for the kids to play in or for the family to enjoy a lovely weekend together. You can spice things up a little bit and add an outdoor pool. Maybe you or your spouse like gardening, which would be perfect in a shipping container home of this design because there is room for more than one garden. As you can see, the smaller containers house the bedrooms and the bathrooms, while the middle one (the biggest) is used for the kitchen, pantry and a lounge where you can watch TV or even have a private study or home office.

Example of open space in a shipping container home.

This spacious design has considered every family member's needs, which makes it ideal for a small or medium family that wants a spacious living area without spending too much money. The catch with a design like this is that you will need to spend some time planning what you want around each section of the house. Making changes after you've started can be difficult, and it will definitely be costly. So, take your time with the design process and make sure every room is where you want it to be. Consider the space and your family's needs. For instance, a lounge might not be a good idea if you have several kids; instead, you can make this into another bedroom. Always think of your future needs, making sure the design is more functional than anything because this counts in the long run.

Plan 3

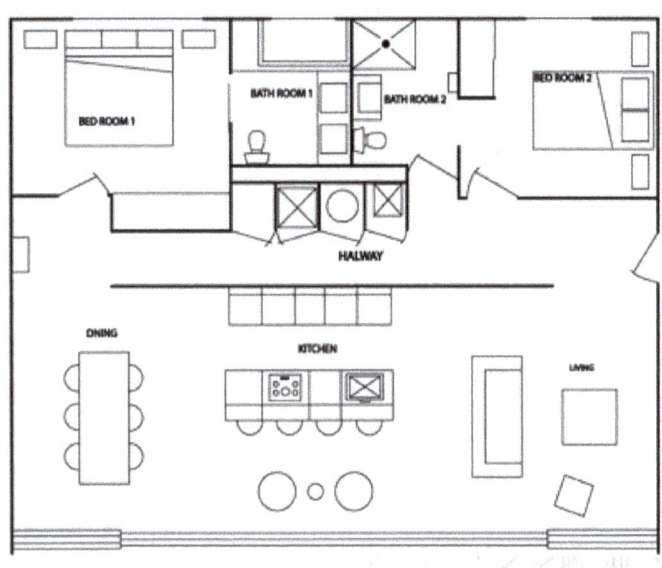

Two containers connected by a wall.

This is an impressive example of a two-container home, and as you can see, the sidewall hasn't been removed from the center of the whole house. The design is simple and minimalistic, yet it makes space for several rooms and spaces around the containers that could prove functional and useful to family members. The hallway is an excellent addition that will make the place feel bigger than it is. It is also helpful that there is enough space for a dining table where the family can eat without feeling crowded—the last thing you want is for the family to feel they live in a cramped space.

Plan 4

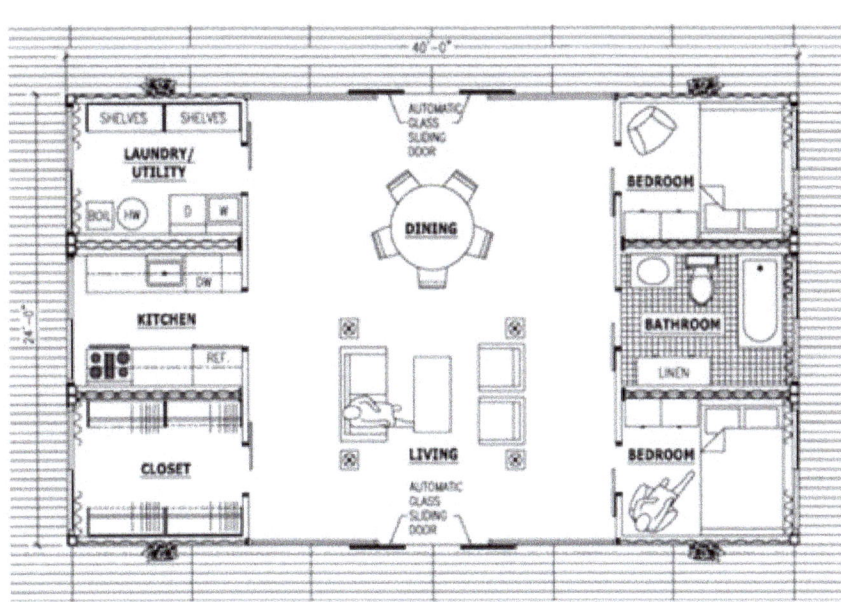

Two containers connected via a wall and with a shed roof.

While this plan might look a bit fuller compared to others, it is also straightforward in nature. It utilizes two containers as well but they're put with some distance between them to make space for the living room and dining table. This open space is walled in by any type of walls you'd like to include, and the plan adds the very cool option of sliding glass doors. Those not only look elegant and are quite the addition to any container home, but they are also functional and easy to use.

Plan 5

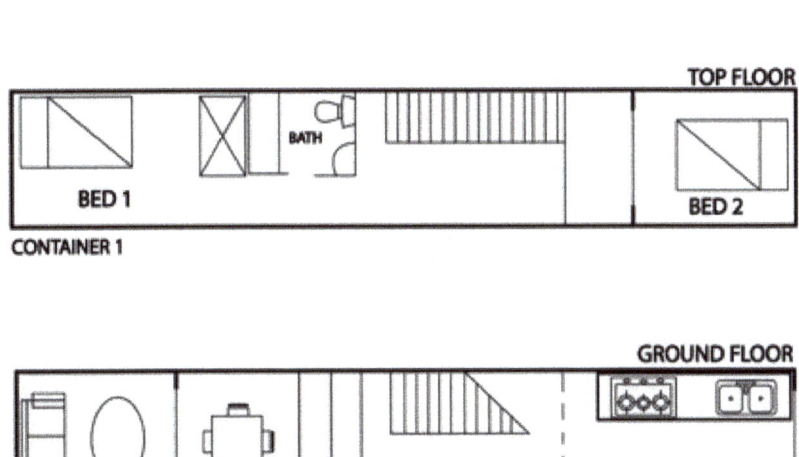

This plan shows a shipping container home with two containers placed over one the other. It looks elegant on the outside, and it's also very functional if your land space is limited and you want to make the most out of it.

Plan 6

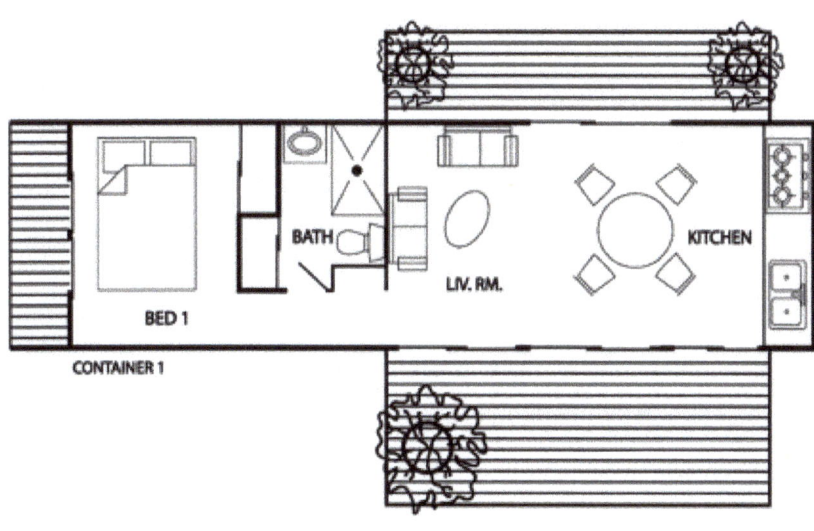

SHIPPING CONTAINER HOMES

This makes the most out of space, being compact and efficient. This home consists of a single container, but the space is efficiently utilized to make room for a bedroom, living room, kitchen and bathroom. This compact living space is ideal for a person living on their own or a couple who wants to create an affordable shipping container home.

Plan 7

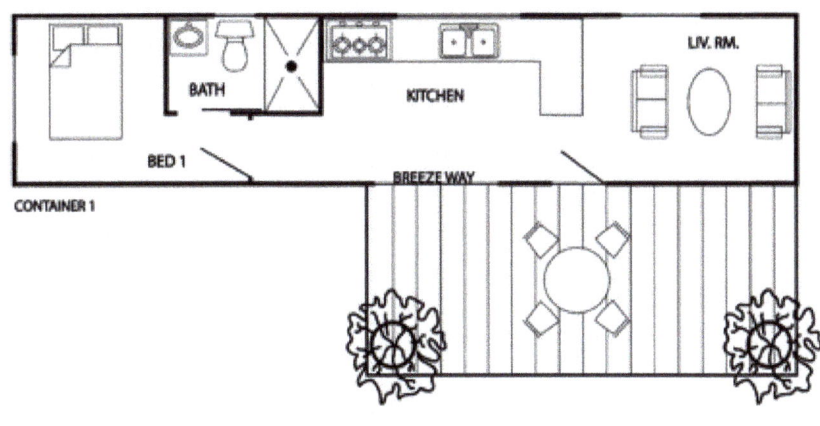

In this plan, the home is also made out of a single shipping container. However, there is room for an outer deck area, which the design utilizes cleverly. You can add a couple of chairs and a table to the deck area and use it for family meals or your morning coffee. It also gives the house quite an elegant facade and the design is stylish and simple.

Plan 8

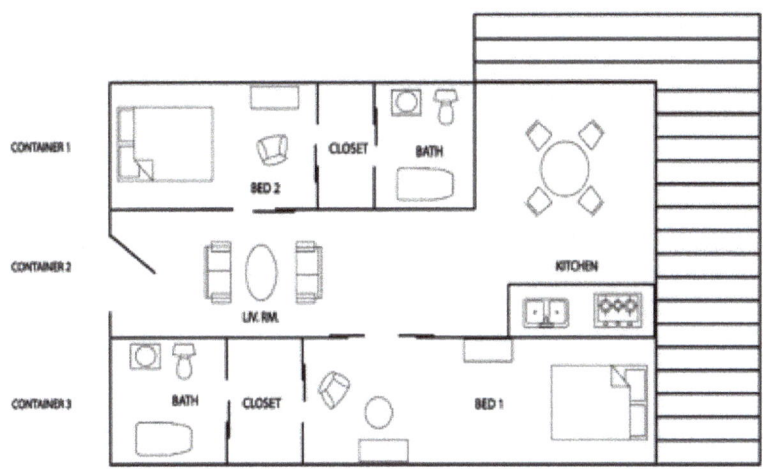

This design utilizes three shipping containers to give the huge space you can see in the plan and the pictures. The first and third containers are used for the bedrooms and bathrooms, while the middle container is used for common areas like the living room, the kitchen and the dining table. With an expanded design like this, you can have space in your shipping container home for any rooms you'd like. Though building such a home won't be cheap—it'll still be much cheaper than a traditional home.

Plan 9

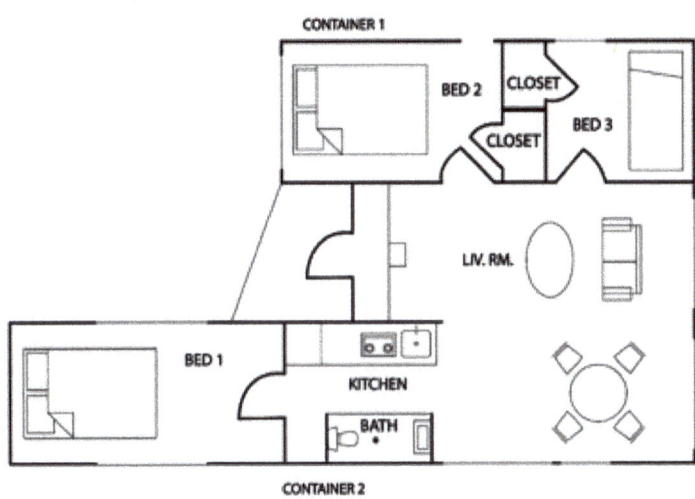

Our next design uses two containers of varying sizes to create this elegant-looking shipping container home. Despite the difference in length, there is still enough room in this home to accommodate three bedrooms, making it ideal for a family. The design also adds several floors to ceiling windows, which, as you can see, are elegant and add to the house's overall style.

Plan 10

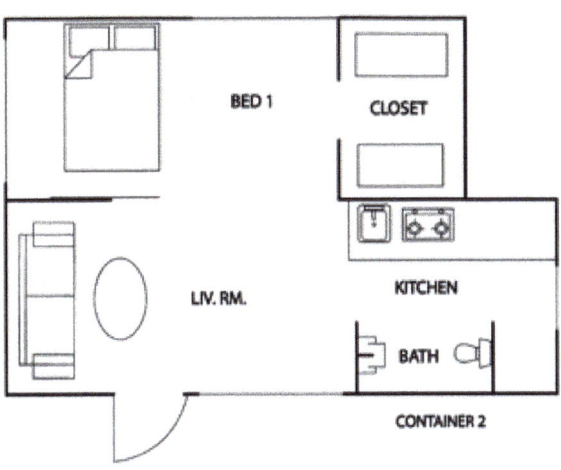

This compact design is for a shipping container home, utilizing two containers of different sizes, as is evident in the images. It has room for one bedroom and a big living room, as well as a bathroom and a kitchen. You could play around with the design if you wanted and change the rooms, but be careful because the space is somewhat limited, so you need to make the most out of it.

CHAPTER 5
Permits and Zoning Laws

Each country and, in most cases, each zoning district within a country has its own zoning regulations. These regulations determine which types of buildings can be placed on a given lot, as well as the density, height and other requirements for structures within the zone. These regulations are complex, and it is not possible to provide all the details for every zone. However, here are a few details that will give some direction in becoming knowledgeable about your country's guidelines. Also included is a list of documents that are likely to be required by any country when designing your home.

Australia

Prior to major building work in Australia, you must obtain a permit from the local council. Check into your state's policy planning framework online and then approach the council to find out the requirements for your state and for the council which governs your intended building site. They will be able to provide you with a list of any documents required for your area or any regulations which should be considered during the design and planning phases.

New Zealand

New Zealand is a bit ahead of the game when it comes to shipping container homes. The Building Act of 2004 offers clear guidance for the construction of these homes. In most cases, they will require building consent, though if they are intended only for storage, then they may be exempt from this requirement. In addition, the territorial authority may choose to exempt your shipping container home from building consent, so long as it still meets the building codes. As in the examples above, the first step is to confer with the territorial authority to look into the specifics of your intended site and design.

United Kingdom

Any construction in the UK will require permission from the local council. The local planning authorities will each have their own specific regulations, so it is necessary to contact them before design and planning. The list of documents provided below will give you a head start and they will be able to inform you if anything further is required.

United States

For most places in the U.S., construction requires a building permit. In order to obtain a building permit, first, contact the local public works department. They will be able to inform you of the zoning status and requirements of your zone. With this information in hand, you can tailor your design to the regulations required.

If your building site is outside the city's zoning code, then it may not require a building permit. If you seek to build without a permit, then deliberately selecting a site outside of the zoning code is one way to avoid a bit of red tape. However, it should be remembered that these sites will have less access to power, water and telephone lines, and will thus present other challenges.

General List of Documents Required

Though each council or local authority will have its own specifications and regulations, here are a few things you can expect to need. Remember that regulations may influence aspects of design, so it still helps to approach your local authority before spending valuable time and energy finalizing your design.

- Structural engineering plans and approval
- Site plan
- Building regulation drawings (to scale)
- Before and after elevations
- Fully dimensioned working drawings

CHAPTER 6
Steps in Building Your Container Home

Site Works

Site works are the first important thing you should do before laying down your foundation. This should also be done before grading work including excavation for utilities, foundations, septic and storm water management. Bring the needed utilities to the site. If needed, you should install a septic system or any storm water management system.

Foundation

The typical foundation is a slab-on-grade application for a three 40-foot container (1,000 square foot) container home design. Make a 24'x40' perimeter from concrete panels (precast), but may be concrete or concrete blocks. For drainage, excavate the perimeter and fill it with gravel. Drop in the precast panels via a crane and these panels should be tied together. These panels have exterior waterproofing membranes and insulation that are factory-added.

Run the utilities (electrical, water and gas lines) to the foundation's base and then to their proper locations as indicated in the plans. After that, back-fill, soil-compact, add gravel, layout reinforcing bars and pour the slab on the foundation walls. Even DIY aficionados would need the help of the general contractor in carrying this procedure out.

Modifications to the Container

Monocoque bodies characterize shipping containers. The corrugated panels (back, sides, and roof), purlins, floors, frame, front doors and rails form a structural skin that is integrated. They are durable and can carry floor loads that exceed what is required in typical home construction. However, when they are modified (penetrating members and cutting holes), they become weak. Thus, it is important to review with an architect or structural engineer, despite the modification level your shipping container home entails.

In removing the container's corrugation along the length of one side, the structural integrity is compromised. The container, with no reinforcement, structurally fails. As a rule, when you take away parts of the corrugated paneling, steel framing should be used to frame out openings. Moreover, roof and column support will be needed depending on the wind/roof loads and the opening's size.

Steel framing, cutting and welding form a large part of the shipping container home's construction and design. Because it is expensive, steel construction is not normally used in the design and use in single-family dwellings and smaller homes. In building container homes and to offset expenses, you should have reinforcing and welding done off-site before putting the containers on-site and commencing interior fit-out. The majority of container resellers can do these modifications. If you plan to make this a DIY project and you do not have the facilities to undergo such a procedure, you should have container modification work done off-site before delivery to your location.

Setting and Securing the Containers to the Foundation

As the modified containers arrive on the site, have them crane-lifted onto the foundation one by one. They should be hooked in place and they should be welded down to integrate them completely with the foundation. Each heavy-gauge container can hold 57,000 pounds and it is also durable. This is why they only have to be fastened to the corners. The container bottom corner blocks are welded to steel plates and are embedded into the slab. This process secures the house to the foundation. The corner blocks are welded into one another to secure containers.

Adding A Roof

You may have or not have a roof depending on how your containers are combined and where you build. If you want to have a home that is not too industrial-looking, a roof would be a nice touch. It is also easy to install a roof, especially since this architectural component is not load-bearing. The cheapest and easiest type of roof to build is a shed roof or a low-pitched gable roof. You should know, however, that the roof should also be insulated and you may need to access the space between the roof and you're ceiling.

Installing Architectural Elements

When the shipping containers were modified offsite, you already have the provision for your architectural elements. The next step for you is to install exterior doors, windows, any skylights and flashing. The windows should be set into the openings that were laid out and cut before the shipping containers were delivered to your site. All openings for doors and windows must be framed with steel sections to regain structural integrity lost through modification. Hollow rectangular sections are good, but L sections also work fine.

Installing Utilities, Fixtures and Floors

On both sides (inside and outside) of the remaining container walls, spray Supertherm insulation coating. Supertherm is a four-part, high-performance ceramic coating and sticks to the shipping containers' steel surface.

You can encapsulate your floor with epoxy and create an extra barrier by installing a sub-floor on top of it. Clean the floors with 91% isopropyl alcohol to remove any acid adhesion or surface oils. Coat the floor with Low V epoxy, which is a Progressive Epoxy Polymers product. The epoxy is not only a physical barrier; it can also protect against vapors from chemical treatments.

Sign-Off and Inspection

Have staged inspections throughout the construction process with the building official and contractor. This means checking on the foundation, electrical and planning, fire safety and architecture. After that, put together for the contractor the final punch list/check. Review this list with your contractor. Afterward, have the building official inspect your newly-finished shipping container home for issuance of the certificate of occupancy.

CHAPTER 7
Buying a Shipping Container

New Or Used?

When you're sourcing your container, one of the first questions is whether you want to go for a brand-new container or a used one. If you choose to go new, then you can request for the floor to be built of safer wood, without the typical pesticides and other toxins. If you pick a used container, you're going to want to inspect it. You have two options here as well. Either choose a single-use container that is unlikely to have taken much damage, or go for an out-of-service container and deal with the rust and dents that come with it.

One-trip containers are the best option to balance value and structural integrity. Plus, you won't have to worry about much rust, mold, or exposure to toxic chemicals. They are usually in better condition than those that have been delivering loads for the last decade. When you convert it into a home, this means a longer life expectancy and reduced construction time. When you're working with something solid, it doesn't take much to shape it how you need it.

At the same time, the budget may be the driving issue. If this is the case, then well-used containers might be preferable. They are often painted with lead paints and treated with pesticides, so you'll need to deal with both issues before considering them safe for habitation. However, with a new floor and a thick coat of spray foam insulation over the interior, these containers could thoroughly transform your living or working area.

When it comes time to inspect the container, here are a few things you'll want to look for:

Rust

When purchasing a used container, you can expect a certain degree of light rusting. However, if there is rusting to such an extent as the integrity of the metal is compromised, find another container. Once again, it's important to check the roof as well when doing your inspection.

Leaks

This is a big one. You don't want a leaky home, and holes that allow water also create openings for other annoyances. Make sure to check the roof of the container and inspect the walls thoroughly. Also, smell the interior of the container to see if you get a hint of mold. This is another indication of possible leaks.

Chemical Contamination

Here's where your nose will really come in handy. You want to smell for anything unusual. Containers may become exposed to pesticides or other chemical hazards when in use. Ask about the history of the container when purchasing, but do a little follow-up yourself to make sure you won't be exposing yourself and your family to chemicals.

Functional Doors and Locks

Make sure to check the doors to ensure that they swing freely, and bolt them to make sure that they fasten securely and that the seal is intact.

Wooden Flooring in Good Repair

It's natural for a container to get a bit banged up when it's in use. However, you want to inspect the wooden flooring to make sure that there are no holes or breakages. Often, the original flooring is covered with a non-permeable layer and used as is, so you may have an additional, time-consuming step in construction if you unwittingly purchase a container with broken flooring.

Intact Identification Code

The shipping container identification code is an 11-digit alphanumeric code inscribed into the container. The history of a container can be tracked with this code, meaning that you can use it to see where it has been and what it has carried. Here is a sample Identification code:

The first three digits constitute the owner code. This identifies the owner of the container.

The fourth digit, the product group code, is a single letter. The only options for this digit are J, U and Z. J indicates that there is equipment attached, Z indicates a container trailer and U indicates a standard shipping container. The remainder of the code is devoted to a six-digit serial number which indicates the precise container and a single number used as a check digit to verify the authenticity of the code. You can use this code to verify information about the container's history.

Where Can I Get One?

The great news is that you can buy a shipping container from pretty much anywhere. Everywhere in the world, you can find disused containers. The key is to find someone reputable. Look into your area with a simple Google search, and you'll be able to find all the best deals in your neighborhood. Just look for "buy shipping containers in…" and you'll find everything you need. Alternately, you can look for "shipping container dealer in…" If the dealer is reputable and the containers look good, you're set.

You know how the internet is. As soon as there is a want, there's a site. So, for all those of you wanting a shipping container, you can go to Green Cube Network. It's a search tool like Skyscanner that checks out all the best shipping containers, factoring in price, distance and anything else you need to consider. It'll clue you into a list of dealers that will have any kind of shipping container you want.

Here's the Green Cube Network link:

http://www.greencubenetwork.org/shipping-container-dealers_3/

If you would like an alternative or you have trouble with GreenCube, feel free to check out eBay, Gumtree, or Alibaba.

What's the Price by Size?

The details are going to vary quite a bit from one supplier to another. Plus, you'll have to look into the condition of the container. As of 2016, these were some pretty good estimates of what you'd be likely to pay for a shipping container:

Dimensions	New			Used		
	U.S.(USD)	Australia (AUD)	U.K.(GBP)	U.S.	Australia	U.K.
20 ft. Standard	$3500	$4000	£2150	$2300	$2900	£1500
20 ft. High Cube	$3500	$4250	£2300	$2400	$3000	£1600
40 ft. Standard	$5900	$7400	£3800	$3000	$3800	£2000
40 ft. High Cube	$6000	$7700	£3900	$3100	$4000	£2100

Pro Tips: You go local because you want to drop the shipping costs as much as possible and because you want to be able to see the goods before they're delivered. Check the container out in person, and you're much more likely to end up with something that you actually want. Plus, by keeping it local, you're stimulating the economy in town around you rather than halfway across the world. Just remember to make the delivery site as close as possible to the foundation.

Remember to get the site prepared before shipping the container. If you've got the foundation in place, the next few steps flow like butter.

Container Purchasing Checklist

- Determine your budget for containers.

- Make any design adjustments necessary, factoring in the price of available containers.

- Decide on new, used, or one-time use containers.

- Source the containers from a reliable local supplier.

- If possible, inspect the container before purchase.

CHAPTER 8
Preparing the Land

Before you can place your container, you'll need to prepare some form of foundation. This will provide a stable, level surface for the container to sit on. While there are three suitable types of foundations, not all local authorities will accept all three and you may have no choice but to use a certain type only. Ideally, you'll want a qualified expert and engineer to lay your foundations as they will know how to deal with soil, codes and the land topography itself. The three main types used for container homes are pile, raft and concrete pier foundations. This is another area where you don't want to compare the shipping container to a mobile home as they are usually much heavier which requires a different type of reinforcement in the concrete.

Foundations

The two most important considerations when laying a foundation are cost and structure. Structurally you need to consult a professional as they will know best about distributing the weight of your container. With softer soil, your foundation needs to be deeper as this adds more stability while hard soil or rock may only require leveling and minor foundation work. There's a tendency to over-spec foundations too which means making them stronger than is strictly necessary simply for peace of mind.

Concrete Piers

These are often similar to what is used for shed and small outbuildings, and they're often the cheapest type of foundation because they require the least materials. In the most basic, these are concrete piers that contain reinforced steel bars that are placed strategically. The steel bars or occasionally steel mesh add to the stability and strength of the concrete. If you are planning on DIYing the foundation, this is the easiest way to go because it requires the least concrete and least scientific approach. These piers should be placed anywhere that the "load" or main weight of the containers will be—the middle and the corners generally. If you're placing more than one container together, you may want to place additional piers at the seams of the two so that both are fully supported. An average of 6 piers per container is standard.

Slab-On-Grade

Raft foundation is significantly more expensive but it's more stable than piers, the reason for this is that the entire container is supported on a concrete raft rather than perched. However, it also requires some digging into the topsoil. The raft foundation is still quite quick to build and is a better idea where temperatures don't drop below freezing much as this lower ground temperature can affect the concrete. It also means that the concrete is prone to getting cold and allowing heat to leach away from your container which is why it's not ideal for cold climates since this will drive up your heating bill. The slab is less affected by bugs and termites as well since there's no wood involved. However, if you're planning on using a slab foundation you MUST have your utilities embedded into the slab and the connections placed exactly to connect with those inside the container since there will be no access to them once the concrete has set and no way to lay them afterward.

Pile Foundation

Similar to concrete piers, these are deeper and more structurally challenging which is why they tend to be the most expensive. This is the type of foundation necessary when your soil is weak and not suitable for a solid slab. There's a great design study with a container home using these called the Graceville Container Home Study which centered around a family whose original home was devastated by flooding and they needed a cheaper rebuilding alternative. Their home was a three-layer 6000ft design that featured everything from a pool and gym to a studio. They needed the deeper piles because of the flood and cyclone risk.

The piles are solid cylindrical steel tubes that are hammered down until they are in more solid ground. Once they are secured, they are filled with concrete and steel rebar which resembles the same as the piers above ground. This is not a construction that can be done DIY because of the need for a pile driver. Since this is the most secure, it is recommended to use this type of foundation anyway if you are doing a multiple stacked design as it will provide extra support.

Strip Foundation

Less common is a combination of slab and pier known as strip foundations. These are strips of thick concrete laid out either on part of the container footprint or around the whole thing. This is a cheaper alternative than a slab but more stable than piers. This is a good choice when the ground is wetter as the inside area being open allows for better drainage. They are, however, less stable than a pile foundation and prone to slippage in high winds or earthquakes since the container can slide. They're quite shallow as well which means they're not suited for stacked container designs.

Concrete

Concrete comes in many grades, and if you've ever looked at the hardware store, you'll see many different types. When it comes to building a foundation, you'll need to use a specific strength of concrete based on your land. The strength is measured in C with a number after it; the higher the number the stronger the concrete. C15 is general-purpose concrete while C30 is a much stronger concrete. C15 uses 1 part of cement to 2 parts of sand and 5 gravel, the amount of cement used increases the strength of the concrete. It's easy to mix small amounts by hand but for piers and slabs, you will need a concrete mixer or to order ready-mix delivered. This does increase the cost of your concrete but it ensures that you don't have one chunk of concrete already dried while you're still mixing it. You must mix it properly together so that it is thoroughly combined or you risk having different structural densities which can cause cracks and weaken over time.

Calculating the amount of concrete needed is fairly simple, you need to know how many square feet your concrete area covers and then mix accordingly. For a 20' container, for example, if you were placing it on a raft foundation that was 2 feet deep and just wider than the container, you would want an area that was 10'x22'x2' or 440 cubed feet of concrete.

When the concrete is mixed, it begins a curing process that eventually hardens and sets it. This typically takes between 5-7 days and requires some moisture to be added to prevent it from drying out too quickly on top and cracking. During the curing period, the weather and temperature need to remain fairly constant and both extreme hot and cold can affect the curing process.

In hot weather, you'll need some form of shade to protect it from direct sunlight and the ground should be sprayed with cold water before pouring. The concrete itself should be mixed with cold water and if possible laid in the evening or early morning to avoid the heat of the day.

In cold weather (below 0°C for three consecutive days), make sure any frost or standing water is cleared from the foundation area first. Then lay the concrete and cover it with an insulating blanket layer immediately. The blankets should remain on for the entire curing time before being removed gradually to raise the temperature slowly and prevent cracking.

Footings

Soil Bearing Capacities

Class of Materials	Load-Bearing Pressure (pounds per square foot)
Crystalline bedrock	12,000
Sedimentary rock	6,000
Sandy gravel or gravel	5,000
Sand, silty sand, clayey sand, silty gravel, and clayey gravel	3,000
Clay, sandy clay, silty clay, and clayey silt	2,000

Source: Table 401.4.1; CABO One- and Two- Family Dwelling Code; 1995.

Within the concrete, you will need footings. These are there to support the foundation and prevent it from settling unevenly and cracking. These are essentially the "feet" that your foundation rests on and are usually 16–20" wide. These are better in good load-bearing soil but if your soil has an uneven distribution, you may have to place different footings across your foundation to make sure it stays solid. When the footing isn't centered properly or the ground is uneven the weight of the building above pushes down and will eventually cause the footing to give way, making the foundation crack. This is almost always determined by an engineer, and even they sometimes get it wrong. The footings are tied very strongly to the type of soil and its bearing capacity.

Footings should be placed a minimum of 6" below where the frost line in the ground is. When the earth freezes, it shifts slightly which means that a footing placed above this line will move with temperature changes. This is especially important if you're planning a shallow foundation. You can find the information for your geographic frost line at the National Snow and Ice Data Center which shows the ground parameters and soil classifications.

The average footing comes in one of three sizes (plus frost line depth):

- 8"x16"x16"
- 12"x24"x24"
- 10"x20"x20"

Each footing is constructed separately usually starting with those which are higher if the design is leveling a slope. The footings are made using 1/2" rebar which is 8" longer than the depth of the concrete. Once the footing hole is dug, the rebar is driven or hammered into the ground so that the top of the rebar is level with the intended top of the concrete. The rebar should be placed every few inches and the amount of rebar will depend on how big your footings are.

Minimum Width of Concrete or Masonry Footings (inches)

	Load-Bearing Value of Soil (psf)					
	1,500	2,000	2,500	3,000	3,500	4,000
Conventional Wood Frame Construction						
1-story	16	12	10	8	7	6
2-story	19	15	12	10	8	7
3-story	22	17	14	11	10	9
4-Inch Brick Veneer Over Wood Frame or 8-Inch Hollow Concrete Masonry						
1-story	19	15	12	10	8	7
2-story	25	19	15	13	11	10
3-story	31	23	19	16	13	12
8-Inch Solid or Fully Grouted Masonry						
1-story	22	17	13	11	10	9
2-story	31	23	19	16	13	12
3-story	40	30	24	20	17	15

Source: Table 403.1; CABO One- and Two- Family Dwelling Code; 1995.

While this table is intended on applying to a standard construction, the load-bearing values compared to the heaviest construction will give you an idea of the expected bearing of each footing. Sometimes, your footings aren't perfect and if it is off-center in good soil, it may not be a problem, however, if the footing isn't centered correctly for the foundation, it will need to be fixed either using gravel, an additional steel tie, or re-augmenting the footing.

If you find you have a soft spot, one where the rebar simply disappears, you may need to excavate and create a pile for that specific footing rather than a pier construction. An alternative is to excavate the soft soil completely and fill the hole back in with gravel or a lower grade concrete. You cannot simply increase the width of the footing without changing the thickness which can cause the concrete to crack.

In fact, there's so much potential that needs to be correct about footings on its own that it could fill a book.

Fixing The Container

Whichever foundation you have chosen; you'll need a solid way of attaching the container. The best way of doing this is by attaching a steel plate into the concrete before it is cured. The steel plate should have vertical bars that sink into the concrete and will add stability. After the curing process has finished, the container can be welded directly onto these steel plates. The plates should be a minimum of 1/4" to 1/2" thick, with thicker plates being stronger. You will still see the top of the plate and this needs to be level across the entire foundation. There are some local codes that apply to this when it comes to metal plates and grades for attachment screws so it's good to do some research if you're DIYing.

An alternative to welding plates is simply to bolt the container directly into the concrete with anchors. This is much simpler and cheaper; however, it is not as strong. You can also use J hooks to attach the container to the exposed rebar in the concrete directly. Concrete anchors are the weakest choice but they can also be an added safety measure if you do these and plate welding.

There is no hard rule about fixing the container to the foundation, and if you're planning on potentially moving the container at a later date, you may choose not to. There is nothing wrong with simply placing the container on top of the foundation but there is a distinct lack of stability and this may affect your home insurance at a later date if it's found to be a factor with damage. Welding makes the containers much harder to remove if you want your home to be portable.

CHAPTER 9
Should You Do It or Let the Professionals?

Purchasing a shipping container to convert into a home does require a certain amount of adaptation, not only to the environment but in regard to amenities. This book is not just about utilizing shipping containers as a shelter against the environment; it's about making your shipping container a home.

In your new home, you'll need a place to sleep, a place to cook and a place to bathe, unless you're going completely rustic.

For these needs, you're going to need plumbing, electricity and hookups for appliances. When it comes to first-timers, it's highly recommended that you find an experienced contractor for your conversion. Doing so will ensure that permits and building codes and safety are followed.

Not all contractors are familiar with shipping container conversions, so take the time to search for one that has some experience in remodeling containers into homes. Search for a contractor based on your needs as similar to those of a person purchasing any property that will become a home.

Following are a few steps that will take the stress out of the entire process. Be aware that finding just the right contractor to work on your shipping container conversion may take a little bit of patience and a lot of asking around.

First, understand the difference between a general contractor and a subcontractor. General contractors are those involved in the entire building process. A general contractor or company can hire subcontractors who specialize in certain aspects of construction/renovations including plumbers, electricians, or even roofers.

Tips for Finding an Experienced Contractor

Tip #1: Have some specific plans for what you're looking for in mind before you even begin your search.

Tip #2: Ask friends, get online, or contact contractors on their websites to see if they've done any contracting for shipping container conversions. If at all possible, you'll want to choose a contractor who has worked on one or more shipping container projects.

Tip #3: If possible, and you live in a populated area, compare experience, potential costs and the feedback or reviews (former clients of two or three different contractors).

Tip #4: Do a background check on your contractor of choice. They should be licensed. Check the Better Business Bureau and perform a general public record check with your local court system to see if any lawsuits have been brought against the contractor or their company. Don't hesitate to request a copy of the contractor's license as well as licenses of any subcontractors he or she brings onto the job.

Tip #5: When it comes to signing a contract, take the time to read every sentence, right down to the fine print. Don't let the contractor rush you. If they're trying to rush you, move on.

Tip #6: Red flags should go up if the contractor states that he or she can get the job done without requiring permits. This is your home; any aspect of your conversion that violates local regulations or ordinances can end up costing you big time.

Tip #7: Negotiate the down payment. In most cases, down payments for a job shouldn't exceed 10% of the overall estimated costs for the project. While budgeting, always allow extra funds for unexpected expenditures—in most cases, 15% extra funds for job completion is adequate—just in case.

Tip #8: Don't hesitate to ask contractors any questions about any aspect of the conversion process. After all, this is going to be your home.

A licensed contractor is required to print their license number on all business cards, contracts and bids. However, always double-check to ensure that their license is currently valid.

Last but not least, the contractor should be covered with commercial general liability insurance. Request to see a copy of their certificate of insurance, or at the very least, their insurance carrier to verify that the contractor is ensured.

Feel Comfortable with Your Decision

In the US, licensed contractors are given a state license number. Visit the contractor's license or reference site to verify that the contractor is properly licensed.

You can do checks on a state-by-state basis to look for:

- Residential and general contractor's licenses
- Electricians' licenses
- Plumbers' licenses
- Utility contractor licenses

The website also provides information about which type of licenses are granted to individuals depending on skill levels. For example, electrical contractors can be divided into three subsections or types of electrical licenses:

- Electrical contractor Class I—this type of contractor is only allowed to work on a single phase of electrical systems of no more than 200 amperes.

- Electrical contractor Class II—unrestricted.

- Low-voltage contractor—can work with one or all the following: alarm systems, telecommunications systems, general systems, or be unrestricted.

About Contractor Bonds

States have different requirements in regard to bonds. A contractor bond protects clients from any work (sub-standard) that doesn't adhere to local building codes.

Note: a contractor bond does not provide any indication of the competency, experience, or honesty of a contractor. Not all states require contractors to carry bonds, but it's common practice for large jobs.

Bonds are classified under three different types:

- Contract bonds—this type of bond insurers and guarantees not only completion of the project/job, but costs and payments for all materials and labor. In most situations, a contract bond is covered for approximately 2% of the contract price.

- Blanket performance and payment bonds—this type of bond stipulates that, based on law, the contractor is not allowed to ask for more than a 10% down payment on the overall contract price of home improvement projects or up to $1,000, whichever is less.

- Contractor license bonds—in most states, a contractor (licensed) carries a $15,000 contractor bond. This is to cover against possible complaints made not only against the contractor but his or her projects.

The key is to research. The more time you take to research during the initial process, the more comfortable you're going to feel with the contractor you choose for your conversion.

Experience is also key. While everyone has to learn somewhere, choosing a contractor who has done a shipping container conversion or two will be much more aware of the potential challenges of the job and will be able to provide options if problems occur.

While it's natural to be anxious for your shipping container to be converted into a home as soon as possible, careful considerations must be taken when looking for and hiring a contractor. Resist the temptation to rush this part of the process.

CHAPTER 10
Insulation

Insulating your shipping container home isn't really a luxury. Whether you live in a hot or cold area, shipping containers can easily transmit heat (or cold) and make your life miserable! There is also the problem of drainage and the possibility that water might leak into the container, whether from its roof or the underside. This is why you have to take insulation seriously and work hard to ensure that your container home is well-insulated. That way, the weather won't be a problem and won't affect your daily life, neither will underwater sources of rainwater.

There are different approaches to insulating shipping containers, and it is trickier than you might think. The main challenge faced when trying to insulate a shipping container is how thin the walls are. Yes, they are sturdy and durable, and they will carry the loads when it is time, but those container walls are also pretty thin, which makes insulation complicated. There is a way around this, but it might mean taking up some of the container's interior space.

Another factor you need to consider while looking for a suitable insulation material is how you plan on building your walls. You will go with different approaches depending on whether you will be adding several containers together; if so, the necessary room for insulation becomes less of a problem. This won't be the case if you're making a snug single or double-container home. In those cases, it is possible to add exterior insulation.

You can use different materials to insulate your shipping container home, whether on the outside or inside.

Cork Insulation

Cork is natural insulation that provides good results. The great thing about cork is that it is renewable and a natural source that is biodegradable since it comes from trees. More important, you don't have to cut down the trees to get the cork. Another significant feature of cork insulation is its acoustic properties, forming an acoustic buffer in your home that will stop sound from leaking outside or coming in from outside. This is particularly important for shipping container homes because those thin steel walls can easily leak sound.

Spray Foam

Spray foam is one of the most popular approaches to insulating containers, and it is one of the fastest ways to do it. The great thing about spray foam insulation is that it's applied to your container's interior and exterior walls. This is useful if your container has been coated with paint that can sometimes have toxic organic volatile compounds added to help the steel survive long periods in the sea. With spray foam insulation, you can contain such compounds and stop them from spreading into your home.

There are different types of spray foam insulation. It is generally a good idea to invest in the best available because it can prolong your home's life, protecting you from several things. Icynene is usually considered one of the best options for spray foam insulation. It is a water-sprayed foam insulation that uses tiny plastic bubbles to fill the insulation's interior, providing excellent insulation and protection. It also doesn't have as many organic volatile compounds as other spray foam products, and those that are there can disappear after only a few weeks.

Wool Insulation

This is one of the natural approaches to insulation, and it also yields good results. Wool insulation is renewable and completely natural, seeing as it comes directly from sheep's wool. This insulation is environment-friendly and quite efficient, providing powerful insulation comparable to denim, fiberglass and other fibrous insulation options. Another great advantage of wool insulation is that it naturally contains lanolin, which is a flame retardant. This means you don't have to treat the insulation with other chemicals for fire protection.

Carefully consider your options before you purchase wool insulation because some types are better than others. Look for companies that sell wool insulation and research the different varieties they offer before settling on a particular type.

Cotton Insulation

Cotton is another natural source of insulation that is environment-friendly and efficient. The advantage cotton offers are that it can be recycled from other clothing sources, so you don't need to source new cotton; pretty great for the environment! Like wool, cotton provides excellent insulation comparable to fibrous insulators like fiberglass. Like wool, boric acid (a natural fire retardant) is usually added to cotton in commercial denim, which means you don't have to treat it for fire protection. The downside to cotton is you have to make sure it doesn't get wet because moisture causes it to lose some of its insulation properties.

Fiberglass

Fiberglass is made from superheated sand and, in other cases, recycled glass spun into thinner fibers. It is cheap wall insulation that is also pretty efficient, so it is very popular in many countries.

Cellulose

Cellulose is loose-fill insulation that relies on adding macroscopic materials in the walls' cavity. The insulating material's chunks are added, but for this insulation, the wall cavities need to be completely contained, or else the material will just spill on the floor. Cellulose is made of recycled paper products that get shredded and then blown into the cavity using a specialized machine.

Factors Affecting Choice of Insulation

Choosing insulation for your home is a major step in this construction process, and you need to take your time and do it right. Insulation is integral to keeping your home at a moderate temperature compared to the outdoors. Each type of insulation has its pros and cons, and you need to consider the advantages and disadvantages before picking a certain type. These are some factors that might affect your choice.

• R-Value: This industry term refers to thermal resistance per unit area. It is a number that expresses how well a material can prevent the transmission of heat. For instance, cotton and wool have an R-value of about 3.5 per inch, which is good. But spray foam has an average R-value of 3.7 per inch—even higher with certain varieties. As you can see, the values differ, and this is a number you need to consider while selecting insulation.

• Performance: The performance of the insulation isn't just affected by its R-value. Other factors come into play, like the open or closed-cell structure of the material (for open-cell foam, R-value is 3.2-3.7 per inch, while for closed-cell foam, it's 6.5-7 per inch), entrapped gas and others. These aspects affect performance characteristics, and you need to consider each before investing in a particular type of insulation.

• Air leakage: good insulation should be able to stop air from flowing through it or around its edges.

• Cost: As with the rest of this shipping container home project, the cost is something that you must consider. This doesn't just include the materials cost and labor and equipment expenses if you won't be able to do it yourself with your tools at home. For instance, spray foam insulation's average cost is around $0.5 per board foot for open-cell spray foam and $1 to $2 for closed-cell spray foam. If you're having professionals install it for you, their time will also be factored in the expenses. Still, spray foam is considered one of the more expensive options compared to the rest. Cellulose costs $1-$1.3, fiberglass is $0.64-$1.2, Rockwool is $0.9-$1.65, cotton is $0.76-$1.4 and wool is $1.33-$2, all per square foot.

• Ease of installation: How easy is it to install this insulation? If it is easy, then you can DIY and save money on labor and equipment. If it is too complicated, you will need help. While the obvious choice is to save money, your shipping containers might need a special type of insulation that will require outside help. Blanket insulation is generally considered the easiest to install and it is available in fiberglass, wood and fibers. On the other hand, spray foam is not as easy and is not recommended for a DIY approach because it requires experience and skills, so you'll most likely have to hire someone to do it for you.

• Net interior space: This refers to how much space remains in your container's interior after applying the insulation—if you applied it on the inside.

• Vapor permeability: Can vapor flow through the insulation? How well does the insulation prevent the vapor from seeping inside and lingering there? Materials like fiberglass, wool and cellulose are considered semi-permeable, while mineral wool is a retarder, as are most foam types, except cementitious foam, which is considered vapor-permeable.

• Sustainability: We mentioned earlier that some insulation types are eco-friendlier than others, which is an important factor to consider for many people. A lot of shipping container homeowners choose sustainability for minimal impact on the environment, so the insulation's sustainability might be a factor to consider.

Types Of Insulation

Wall and Ceiling Insulation Application

When you think about insulating your shipping container home, you have to think about what approach you want to follow—interior, exterior, or both. Considering that shipping container homes are basically metal boxes; they are excellent conductors of heat. So, the best approach will be to insulate both the interior and the exterior of the container for the best results. This is especially important if you live in extreme weather conditions where choosing just one type of insulation would lead to heat control problems in your home.

External Insulation

The concept of external insulation is simple. If you don't have it, the container will easily heat up. Relying just on the internal insulation will lead to heat or cold seeping through internal insulation, affecting your entire living situation. This applies to both summer and winter, and things will be much worse if you suffer from extreme seasonal changes where you live. In short, external insulation will help keep the home cool in summer and warm in winter. This also means it will reflect on your energy expenditures; you'll save on heating/cooling costs with proper inside and outside insulation.

Another cool feature of external insulation is that it can help improve your shipping container home's outer facade. One approach that some people follow is filling the voids of the corrugated container wall with insulation, spray foam most likely, and after that, it will be ready for paint or cladding. This is, however, a somewhat more expensive option that might not work with all budgets.

It is also important to insulate the container's underside because a lot of heat and moisture might seep in or out from there. The best time to do that is when placing your container on the foundation. If that doesn't work, you have another option of adding insulation underneath the flooring. In any case, make sure there is some form of insulation on the underside of the container.

While we recommend insulating both the interior and the container's exterior, some people prefer saving inside space by only exterior insulation. Not modifying the container's internal walls does preserve a lot of floor space, but you need to make sure your external insulation is done properly. Exterior insulation will help you preserve that floor space while providing some heat control. Remember that you will also need to insulate your container's roof, whether you are leaving the original roof or adding a new one.

If you add a new roof, adding spray foam or other insulating materials underneath it should be fairly easy. If you leave the roof as it is, you need to cover it in an insulation layer. This is particularly important if you don't plan on adding a ceiling inside the container since this means you won't be adding the interior insulation that comes with the ceiling—this one doesn't take up any extra height. In other words, if you don't plan on adding a ceiling, make sure the roof is well insulated.

Internal Insulation

Many people ignore internal insulation, thinking it is not really essential, but it can make a world of difference. While external insulation does the biggest job in controlling the heat or cold seeping into the shipping container, climate may still make it past that first layer; this is where internal insulation comes in. To partition and frame your container's interior, then adding insulation won't take up much space, and the same goes for when you add a new ceiling. Suppose you leave an exposed ceiling (the container's original). You should expect rust after a while since there will be a lot of condensation inside the container and affect the original steel ceiling.

The great thing about spray foam insulation inside your house is it can help you improve the place's aesthetic value. It can cover up any dents or scratches or any other marks on the walls, and it is easy to paint over spray foam insulation. You can use external insulation or internal in certain places, or you can double up in areas such as the roof/ceiling to minimize any heat seeping into your home.

CHAPTER 11
Utilities

G etting services on your site is not just essential to make it easier for you to live in your container house. You are expected to use items like pumps, water tanks and port-a-potties without facilities.

Although any organization has to be contacted on its own, resources, such as In My Area, help demonstrate which businesses (through different kinds of services) serve your place.

One factor to verify is whether all of the utilities have a minimum monthly fee. If so, we will suggest that you wait until you are able to start building the hook-up. If you do it early, you just have to pay the bill, regardless of when you ever need it.

Depending on where you are, certain services can be deregulated, monopolized easily by a corporation, or governed by the government. If you have an option between several firms providing the same utility service as a customer, make sure to do some homework to figure out which fits better for your case.

You should also verify if they have any energy-saving benefits or rebates that you might have on your template with just a few tweaks. Even utilities provide you with a financial opportunity to use quality insulation and windows, more energy-friendly equipment, etc. Make sure you ask!

Electricity

Electricity is the first and perhaps most significant utility. To figure out the method of installing an electric meter and linking power, you will have to call your nearest electric utility and cooperative.

If you have power lines on the main road near your property now, you should be in a position to add electrical service. The concern as to how much it costs will depend on such factors as installing a new transformer, how long (and difficult) it will be from a run and whether it will go underground or on poles.

Normally, the firm provides you with a certain gap between the wire and the poles, and you must then compensate the extra distance above that number. You should be able to get an appreciation. Understand that in many situations, you get a discount on the real costs to install it in the belief that you will benefit from your annual subscription charge over time.

This makes it possible for the electrical provider to see some success before they undertake to expand the electrical supply to your site. If they are less than sure that they can ever complete the container home and be a happy client, they will reserve the right to pay for the installation. Or you can pay for a greater share to reduce this chance. Each business is different, so make sure that you figure out what people in your field need.

Understand that permits and permissions are necessary, especially for additional overhead poles that can affect neighbors. You may not have to start the installation immediately on our preceding stage, but you can contact them as soon as possible to clarify the procedure and the timetable involved.

You probably want to get temporary power mounted first as part of this operation, which provides you with some electric circuits. It should be enough to build, but too little for the whole building. The business will return later after the completion of the house and have your permanent service mounted.

If you do not find commercial electricity, it might be more appropriate to live off of the grid with a battery, wind turbine, or solar panels than to pay the electricity provider to expand their access to you.

Gas

Gas is perfect for space heating, stoves which water heaters, and usually requires natural gas or propane. If you're in the area, you can reach the natural gas line that you can tap with one meter like electricity.

In more rural areas, you can typically buy or rent a large gas tank that meets your needs month after month.

The easiest thing to find out about the petrol prices in your area is to make educated decisions about the types of equipment that you choose to have in your home. In general, if gas is affordable, it is the cheapest and simplest to use.

Sewer And Septic

If your property provides access to local sewage pipes, the cost and method of binding must be identified. A septic system is probably your only choice for more remote areas.

The first cost of installing a septic system would typically be much higher than a sewer connection, but after completion, it cost virtually nothing, compared with the monthly cost of your sewage connection.

Most septic systems have buried tanks and lines of leach pipes or sprinklers. Work with your installer to create a good place for this equipment that does not damage future work or livelihood.

Telecommunications

While some people are constructing container houses in rural areas to get away from anything, most people want to have some access at least. The choices available will differ significantly from place to location.

In the area, you will have many ways to bundle TV, Internet, or even telephone services into one bill, including cable, DSL and fiber. Outside the capital, satellite devices, slower speed cable/DSL links, or even earth-to-point radio frequency equipment may be used to obtain these services.

If you have access to several choices, make sure that you call and match rates and haggle. We would like to talk to neighbors about the solution they use and if they like it.

Telecommunications connectivity can be useful, for example, to tie up surveillance camera tracking and to make Google searches or internet shopping available quickly from the web!

Water

Water is last but not least. The same drinking water you bathe with in the United States is also your drink, while in other countries, you will have to prepare to buy drinking water separately.

In any case, all but most remote sites normally have access to sewage. If you can't get affordable access, you would either have to pay to dig a well or to get water trucked into and kept in a tank on-site.

All these solutions have higher initial costs but will be reasonably rational if you intend to own the container for the coming years.

CHAPTER 12
Installation of Doors and Windows

Shipping container doors and windows can be added to just about any kind of shipping container.

After your container has arrived and been settled and anchored to the foundation, it's time to focus attention on other details. Do you want windows? You'll need a door, unless of course, you want to use the original cargo hasp and latch the original door to the container. Most don't.

Cutting out a few windows and a doorway is not going to damage the integrity of your steel container—if done properly—but do be aware of placement. A few things to consider:

- Cross ventilation—in warmer months, you want to encourage the movement of air through the container which can provide relief against hot temperatures.

- Exposure to the elements—too many windows can make it more difficult to maintain a comfortable ambient temperature inside your container, especially in cold winter months or blazing hot summers.

Determining the location of windows and doorways is essential before beginning to work on interior design, especially if you plan on installing insulation, drywall, or paneling. How you decide to divide the container into separate living or usage spaces will also have an influence on where you place windows, as well as their size.

Note: Be aware that, depending on the size and number of containers you're using to construct your new home, building codes may stipulate a certain number and size of windows for any portion of the space. Always check with your local building department for information regarding ventilation, accessibility and dimensions of windows.

In some rural or sparsely populated areas in the US, city zoning laws may not be applicable, but always research first.

Tip: Always apply for needed permits when it comes to not only placement, foundation and/or construction of a container home, but smaller details such as:

Installation Requirements

- Roofing requirements (and slope of the roof depending on geographical location)

- Number and dimensions of windows based on the size of space

- Plumbing codes

- Electrical codes

Obtaining permits before you do anything can save you thousands of dollars. Better safe than sorry!

Planning for Windows and Doorways

As mentioned, steel containers are incredibly strong. It takes a lot to damage them or weaken their structural integrity. However, excessive modifications can cause problems down the line.

What does that mean? It means using discretion and common sense when planning for the number and size of windows and doorways for your home.

If you cut out large sections of steel, it stands to reason that you are going to weaken the structure, especially when these large sections are cut out of the longer sides of the container home.

Stacking containers on top of each other may require special considerations in regard to windows and their size.

In order to prevent structural damage, be prepared to spend money on reinforcing these areas with steel beams that must be welded in place, which can be expensive and time-consuming.

This is not to say that you have to forgo your views or your wish list when it comes to the size of your windows, but do be aware that depending on the location, additional support—and associated increases in cost—will have to be considered.

Can I Put in a Sliding Glass Door?

Sure! However, be prepared to custom order a sliding window for your new container home depending on the desired size. Sliding doors are typically constructed of either corrugated or heavy-duty steel. Modifications to the container may be required (referring to the potential for additional support beams).

A number of businesses focusing on shipping container modifications when it comes to doors and windows are popping up more often on the Internet. One of the more popular is CubeDepot.

You'll have to make a decision whether your shipping container sliding glass window is constructed of single steel or double steel. Sizes also differ, but are most commonly found in:

- 14x7 feet
- 3x7 feet
- 10x7 feet

You'll have to also decide whether you want an external or internal sliding door or window. The external sliding door utilizes rails supports and a trolley system on the outside of the shipping container. The internal sliding door rolls and slides (and locks) on the inside of the container.

Doorways

You'll also have a number of options when it comes to doorway selections. Again, it's a matter of preference, but it's recommended that you confer with a professional contractor and window/door specialist to ensure the maintained integrity of the container.

Following are two popular options for shipping container doorways:

Rollup Door

A rollup door is an option and operates much like an electric garage door opener or the type of door you find on storage units. Most of these measure between 4 feet and 10 feet in width and approximately 7 feet in height. They're constructed with sliding lock clasps such as those found on storage units and are constructed with 26-gauge galvanized steel—colors may be optional.

Heavy-duty rolling doors are typically available in widths ranging from 4 feet to 8 feet wide, and as the standard roll-up doors, are usually 7 feet in height. They are manufactured from anodized metal aluminum. They're also watertight and come with manual key locks.

Traditional Residential Door

A traditional residential door looks much like the door on any home in neighborhoods across the country; typically, 3 feet wide and 6.5 to 7 feet in height. Of course, custom-made doors of different dimensions are always possible but will cost more.

A traditional residential door is typically constructed of wood and covered with metal skin. All-steel doors are also an option. When contacting a local door company in regard to options, ask about deadbolts, overhead drip ledges and handle locks.

For those concerned about enhanced security, security swing arms may also be installed on any traditional residential-sized door. The security swing arm is typically manufactured with 1"x2" steel tubing. A lockbox is welded onto the end of the arm that fits over the door. This way, exterior locks can't be removed with bolt cutters.

Let's Talk Windows

Visit any retail home supply store like Home Depot or Lowe's and you'll find dozens of options for windows. Before choosing, again refer to your local building regulations in regard to ventilation based on square footage as well as size.

Windows can be pre-ordered and cut to specifications based on your needs. Windows can be fitted with:

- Screens
- Protective covers
- Security bars

Popular window sizes for container homes average:

- 2'x3'—narrower dimensions' top and bottom with windows sliding up and down
- 3'x3'—left to right sliding

Note: Do-it-yourselfers cutting holes into the side of the shipping containers need to be aware that if the square is not cut perfectly, the window won't fit. Proper framing and installation are essential.

Do-it-yourself instructions on the Internet suggest a number of methods for cutting out windows in the side of your shipping container. Not all are recommended!

The two most common methods for cutting window openings:

- Torch
- Angle grinder

A do-it-yourselfer should also be aware that the process involves:

- Dry fitting the frame into the opening
- Ensuring that everything is level and plum
- Tack-welding the frame
- Grinding welds smoothed
- Caulking (some use black urethane windshield adhesive, though other do-it-yourself instructions may recommend other caulking material)

You may need to weld your own door hinges and angle irons as well as security bar frames, depending. All pieces must align properly for the insertion of bolts.

Tip: Don't caulk until the hinges and any other security iron or angle iron pieces have been welded because the heat from the torch will damage the caulking.

Last but not least, insert a premade window into the frame (unless windows are pre-manufactured and come in a ready-to-install unit).

Can I Put a Skylight in My Container?

Yes, you can! However, be aware that installing a skylight (regardless of size) into the top of a metal shipping container is slightly different than installing one in a traditional home.

A number of considerations must be factored into size, shape, materials. For example, some are made of aluminum and are pre-assembled with flashing before installation.

Note: Always be aware of the need to drain excess water around the base of any skylight. Even on a sloped roof, skylights can leak if not sealed properly. It is recommended that if interested in a skylight, angling can reduce leaking or puddling issues.

That being said, before ordering skylights of any type, determine which type is more suitable for a flat roof or a pitched roof.

One popular manufacturer for tubular skylights is ODL. This type of skylight is constructed with a rooftop dome that catches and then funnels light through a reflective tube into the ceiling, where light is diffused.

The "tube" construction can be simplified and height adjusted/modified for use on shipping container homes. Such tubular construction offers economical and efficient natural light solutions:

- 10-inch skylight—illuminate up to 150 ft.^{2}
- 14-inch skylight—illuminate up to 300 ft.^{2}

Of course, other manufacturers and brands are available. Compare pricing and diffuser options. The tubular skylights mentioned above are suitable for sloped metal or corrugated materials as well as flat roofs.

It is recommended—unless you have experience cutting windows and doors in shipping container homes—that you confer with a construction expert and pay for someone who has done it before to install windows and doors. Making a mistake cannot only ruin the integrity of your structure but lead to unsightly damage that can contribute to the additional outlay of money.

While you can certainly find do-it-yourself instructions on websites like YouTube and Pinterest, get a quote on how much it will cost to have your windows and doors professionally installed. It may cost a little more than doing it yourself, but having a licensed contractor do the job will ensure that it's done right, will be up to code and will reduce the possibility of mistakes.

CHAPTER 13
Designing Your Home

Exterior Design Ideas

When it comes to the exterior design of your new home, the sky's the limit. Because of their solid steel structure, they are quite often stronger than a traditional house. Containers weigh on average around 8000 pounds and are designed to hold up to 57,000 pounds inside without any risk of damage. However, your design plans can be compromised if you decide to do a lot of cutting on the exterior structure without replacing that support in some form or another.

Therefore, there is quite a bit of preparation of the exterior of the structure needed before you can even begin to think about the inside. When designing the exterior of your house, you have to plan for laying a foundation, cutting and reinforcing openings for doors and windows. You will also need to incorporate your ideas for the roof and the flooring.

- Foundation: There are at least three different types of foundations you can choose from.

- Concrete: concrete block foundation is the most budget-friendly and the easiest to lay. They are strong and can easily support the weight of a loaded container, especially if you design welded corners and steel reinforcements to secure the container in place.

- Crawl Space: Designing a crawl space for the foundation is a great option if you're in need of extra storage space but they aren't as strong as the concrete foundation.

- Basement: In some areas, a basement is a good idea but this type of foundation will depend largely on the water table, the type of soil you have and the bedrock found in your location.

When designing foundations, make sure you speak to an architect that is familiar with the building codes and regulations that may apply.

- The Cuts: The next phase of the exterior design is deciding where to cut for the doors and windows. Again, because of the sturdy construction of the steel box, you need to know exactly where to cut and how much so you don't compromise the integrity of your structure.

Finally, you want to design the roof and the flooring of your container. In most cases, if you've made a wise decision on buying a One-Trip container, the floor will already be in good condition. These floors are super strong and can handle the extra weight you might need to add and are weather tight. On the other hand, the roof is another matter entirely. Often, there is no design for water run-off for containers in inclement weather. As a result, the water pools on the top and you may find a great deal of corrosion that needs to be repaired.

To deal with that problem, you may have to weld a new roof in place. And if you plan to use solar energy, the panels are usually installed into the roof design for better efficiency.

When all the designs are laid out for the exterior of your new home you have one more step before you can begin the serious construction phase. The entire container will need to be thoroughly cleaned and sterilized to ensure your family's safety. This is because you do not know what materials were earlier shipped in the container. The residue left behind from chemicals or toxins could still be lingering on the floor or the walls of the container. It is recommended that after a deep cleaning that the floor is covered with an epoxy or polyurethane coating to seal off any possibility of gases that may escape later on.

Interior Design Ideas and Modifications

One of the great things about shipping container houses is that they can be built to be whatever you want. A single container can easily be developed into a tiny house or even a starter house for a single person or a couple. However, if by chance you want to grow your family, adding on a second, third, or fourth container can give you the added space without the exorbitant costs.

You have the option to go big or small. For example, if you aren't interested in a lot of space, you can choose a small single container structure that can be situated either on the grid with all of the amenities a city has to offer or completely off the grid. This small container home has only 107 sq. ft. of living space, which is great because in many places a home that size does not require any special building permits. The home is fully equipped with just the basics and it set the homeowner back only about $24,000 USD.

For space-saving design features, consider designing built-in multi-purpose furniture. This way, your home will have as many functions as it needs but storage space will not be an issue.

It is also important to consider height. Unlike a standalone house, container homes have a definite height measurement that usually falls between eight and nine feet. Keep this in mind if you plan on designing loft space, you'll either have to cut out part of the roof to expand or you'll need to purchase a second trailer for upper floors.

Take advantage of using glass for the windows and doors. This will give a feeling of more space even when you're limited. A strategically placed sliding door can give your home the feel of blending with the outdoors environment and giving you more space as well.

Clear light roofing can also bring in a lot of natural lighting into your living space.

Finally, you want to make sure that you have a large enough water storage system to ensure that you don't run out of water to meet all of your needs.

CHAPTER 14

Success Stories

You can read through this entire book, but don't only take it from us. Read through stories of how people have successfully managed to build a new life for themselves in a shipping container.

One of the first home projects to hit mainstream was the Simon's Town High School Hostel. The project was intended to create affordable housing for students. The company Safmarine donated 40 used shipping containers to the school, which set to work immediately. With the 40 units in total, the building can house up to 120 people. Back in 1998, this cost them a total of $227,000. It opened on November 27th and is still open to this day. At the time of its creation, the hostel was the largest structure ever to be built using shipping containers and the success of the project paved the way for others in the future.

Solution to Housing Problems

Shipping container homes might just be the answer to the worldwide housing problem. This is not an exaggeration, having appropriate living quarters is a fundamental human right; however, between building costs skyrocketing, cities getting overpopulated and the housing market being so unstable, there are a lot of people who are homeless through no fault of their own. Building shipping container housing projects might just be the answer, especially with China producing so many one-trip containers that end up taking up space in docks everywhere in the world.

The shipping container housing project in Brighton was deemed an overwhelming success and cost half of what it would have cost if it had been a regular housing project. It provided homes for homeless people in the area, thus allowing them to get back on their feet. If the movement catches on as a global trend, there is a big chance that these sorts of housing projects start appearing in every densely-populated city.

In Orange County's Midway City, a similar housing project took on, only this time it was specialized for housing homeless veterans. This is a test project so the build only included 16 residences. This housing project is the first of its kind in America and while it was hard to get the necessary permits to start the build (which is an unfortunately prevailing problem with building shipping container homes), what ended up convincing the housing authorities was just how cheap and sustainable the project itself was. It is hard to build housing projects that are both environmentally friendly and cost-effective, so far, the only option available that offers both things are shipping container homes. It is quite impressive for something that has been deemed a "passing fad."

Containers Of Hope

In 2011, the world saw just how ingenious the use of shipping containers could be when a house in Costa Rica was built for only $40,000. Containers of Hope was designed and built by architect Benjamin Garcia Saxe, who worked closely alongside his clients for the project.

The house is built using two shipping containers together, and the roof of one has been raised to let in airflow due to the hot temperatures of Costa Rica. It is built on raised cement platforms, just outside the city.

The amount of money spent only refers to the construction and not the gorgeous design of the interior, but it still speaks volumes about how cheaply you can build a home with shipping containers. Remember, this was made with two shipping containers, not one, and still managed to stay on a fair budget.

(Photo by Andres Garcia Lachner of Studio Saxe)

They make use of natural light through the windows to make the space feel more open. You can see here, again, how the pieces that were cut out have been repurposed and added elsewhere to the structure.

Social Housing

While building the Containers of Hope, it came to the attention of the people in the production that it was costing them less to build this house than it was to build the social housing in Costa Rica. This sparked an interest in governments around the world, questioning whether these shipping containers were the answer to economic housing. This is where most people have the idea of shipping container homes as the apartment complexes of the future. It seems to present itself as the solution to all the world's housing problems, and in some recent novels that have settings in the near future, we can see this idea of stacked shipping containers being the primary method of housing. For example, the popular novel "Ready Player One" by Ernest Cline sees the lower class in stacked homes that echo the shipping container aesthetic.

But when brave, slightly brazen architects present their ideas, it is never as a lower class dystopian "stacks," but as a bright futuristic building where containers are laid out, some sticking out, sometimes creating a building that looks as if its walls are in motion. These ideas are striking, certainly, but don't always reflect reality. For example, many of these proposed buildings fail to consider the structural integrity of shipping containers—for example, that cutting windows will weaken the walls and would cost to reinforce, and that if they are stacked too high, the weight will crush the ones below.

But for some governments, this idea was too good to pass up on, and projects have begun to take place. In the city of Vancouver, Canada, shipping containers were used to build a small, cheap housing complex for women in their downtown area. The complex is made up of 12 containers. It houses women who had before been living in shelters, or out of hotel rooms. The project was completed in 2015 and was a great success. Though it is only a small complex, baby steps forward are steps nonetheless, and Vancouver again looked forward to what it could do with shipping container homes. In 2017, Vancouver modified over 20 shipping containers into modular housing, made specifically for the city's rising homeless population. Vancouver is known for its biting winters, and the goal of the project is to shelter the homeless throughout those cold winter months.

Vancouver is the first in Canada to attempt a project like this. Hopefully, if it is successful, these modular houses can become permanent homes and more cities across the world can begin building in their image.

Six Oaks

Down in sunny California, Studio Modulus created a beautiful structure near a historical trail. Called "Six Oaks" for the six recycled shipping containers it uses, the house makes use of perpendicular stacking. The interior was made from recycled parts wherever it could and boasts a fireplace to add to the rustic feel.

As you can see, the structure makes use of the hillside for its top floor, supporting the outside container with a cement pillar. This is more a success story in saving the environment as in saving money; having set out to build a structure with as small a carbon footprint as possible while proving that you do not have to sacrifice style or ingenuity.

The 12 Container House

It would be a travesty to talk about stories of success and not mention the 2003's masterpiece: The 12 Container House. This fascinating piece makes use of, as the title implies, 12 shipping containers together. Unlike Vancouver's modular housing complex for women, however, this house has most of the inside walls cut away. Two grand staircases lead down into the wide-open living room, while bedrooms are stacked on the far sides. The house itself is something of a T-shape, with the containers lying horizontally to the back, while to the front, they are placed vertically.

All in all, architect Adam Kalkin estimated the price came to about $125 per square foot, unbelievably low for something that looks so luxurious.

You can see in the 12 Container House, an example of adding a rooftop. Keep in mind for your own projects, though they will not likely be 12 container mansions such as this one, your added rooftop may look a little something like this.

There are more wonderful stories of people who have learned to use shipping containers, but they are not always shared. Most of the people who build shipping container houses for the sake of being noticed are architects, who want to experiment with styles and be noticed. Plenty of people are building homes with shipping containers every day and not getting any media coverage for it. If you want to, take a walk around the downtown area of your city and keep an eye out for any shipping container homes. The chances that you see one, or a few, are higher than you think. Talk to the people who built them, or even if they bought them prefabricated, listen to their story. Learn from their experiences.

CHAPTER 15
Frequently Asked Questions

Just like any other topic in the world, there are certain questions that are commonly asked all the time. We will talk about some of the frequently asked questions in this so that your journey of building a shipping container home gets easier.

Is There a Chance of Getting Baked Inside a Shipping Container Home in Hot Weathers?

Well, the answer is no. Generally, any kind of structural base, be it concrete, wood, steel panels, or blocks, have the chance of getting hot in higher temperatures. Every structure needs proper ventilation and insulation. As long as you can maintain proper insulation and ventilation of your shipping container home, you will not have any kind of problems related to temperature regulation.

In Which States Can I Build Shipping Container Homes?

Some of the states that are the most receptive for shipping container homes are:

- California
- Missouri
- Louisiana
- Alaska
- Texas
- Tennessee
- Oregon

The majority of the states will allow you to build shipping container homes; however, the governing authorities will determine the requirements and regulations. Make sure you schedule lots of project time as the approval process for container homes might be longer than traditional homes.

Will My Shipping Container Home Rust and Corrode?

Remember that shipping containers are built for the transportation of goods across the ocean. It indicates that they are designed for saltwater and humidity. Shipping containers are built from special kinds of steel that are non-corrosive. They also come with a ceramic coating that makes them rustproof virtually. So, it can be said that your shipping container home will not rust and corrode with proper care.

Will My Shipping Container Home Hold Any Value?

There is no form of any historical data of the market that can help in estimating the appreciation or depreciation of any shipping container home. In order to properly hedge the risk of depreciating asset, you will have to place the containers at a place that have chances of appreciating with time. Container homes generally involve some degree of risk because of: shorter lifespan, chances of rust, feature and size limitations, and also competitive alternatives. As a shipping container home ages, it might tend to be less desirable for prospective buyers. You can get in touch with a local agent, specifically if shipping container homes are prevalent in the area.

Is Any Permit Required for Building a Shipping Container Home?

While building a container home, you will require permits for all those things that you generally need for any kind of traditional buildings. But before you get your land, try to check with the county or city authorities to determine if there is any restriction or requirement to develop a shipping container home. Make sure that you opt for experienced shipping container home contractors or engineers to adhere to the best practices. Before your shipping containers reach the building site, you need to get done with these tasks – land purchase, building permits, and construction of the foundation. Restrictive zoning and planning boards might need a site survey, structural engineering reports, and architectural design review before you can start with any kind of actual construction. In case your county does not have much experience with shipping container homes, you can expect repeated visits and delays before getting a green signal.

Are Container Homes Sustainable?

Some of the reasons why shipping container homes cannot be regarded to be sustainable are:

- **Premature recycling:** Used containers often get recycled too soon as there are various homes that are built with only single-use containers.

- **Remnant toxins:** The majority of the shipping containers get treated with toxic paints along with toxic chemicals for the flooring to maintain durability. Also, there are containers that carried toxic cargo.

- Inefficient recycling: One shipping container, if only recycled as steel, can yield plenty of metal studs for building fourteen houses of the exact same size in comparison to container homes.

- COR-TEN steel: There are shipping containers made from COR-TEN steel, which has lots of environmental baggage, along with corrosion and rust.

As most of the shipping container homes that you can find are made with used containers, there are industry practitioners who see this as a type of upcycling. But this form of upcycling is quite inefficient, provided the reasons above.

Can Shipping Container Homes Turn Out to Be Toxic?

The sole purpose of shipping containers is to transport goods for as many trips as they can. In order to improve their durability, containers are often treated with toxic chemicals. They are not really manufactured for being used as living spaces. Also, the containers might get used for the transportation of toxic goods. The paint used on the walls is very tough and contains loads of chemical compounds that someone would not want in their house. It is always suggested to sand down the existing paints, down to the layer of the raw steel. You can also add extra layers on the walls and floors for sealing the toxic materials.

Do I Need to Get a Foundation for My Shipping Container Home?

Yes, you will need a proper foundation for your container home for two reasons.

- You cannot allow steel to touch the ground as the moisture from the ground might lead to rusting.

- The shipping container needs to be placed on a stable and non-shifting base.

Is Shipping Container Home a Bad Choice?

Generally, shipping container homes are suggested when you have a tight budget. But they are often considered to be bad investments for having:

- Minimal cost saving

- Short lifespan
- Fewer options of financing
- Small spaces for living
- Reduced integrity of the structure
- Long approval and permitting processes
- Limited option for future changes or modifications

Whether you want to get a shipping container home or not can be easily determined by going through all the above-mentioned answers.

CHAPTER 16
Sustainable Living with Your Shipping Container Homes

Interior design aside, you need to think about ways to improve your shipping container home's sustainability. One of the most important reasons many people invest in such homes in the first place is how they can be used to reduce carbon emissions of a residential home, not to mention live off the grid with minimal damage to the environment.

Contrary to popular belief, while container homes are better than traditional ones in terms of environmental friendliness, not all shipping container homes are necessarily eco-friendly. Your practices determine just how sustainable your shipping container home can be, and there are things that you will need to do to make sure that your shipping container home is environment friendly.

Appliances

Electrical appliances around the house are one of the areas in which you can seriously reduce your carbon footprint and minimize emissions. For starters, we leave a lot of devices on or on standby, which results in wasted electricity and all the harm that comes with that. It is obviously easier for us to leave devices on standby mode to turn on quickly, but it is wasteful. This is why a better approach would be turning these devices off when you are not using them, whether that is done by unplugging the machine or turning off switches.

You might think that standby devices don't necessarily consume too much power, but you would be mistaken. Studies show that at least 10% of residential electricity consumption is done through standby devices, which is huge. So, reducing energy consumption and being sustainable is definitely worth waiting a few extra seconds or even minutes until the device powers on.

Moreover, if sustainability is something you care about, you should also start considering investing in eco-friendly appliances, and there are many options. You can get an Energy Star-labeled refrigerator that minimizes electricity consumption in your shipping container home. You could also consider switching to a gas oven instead of an electricity-operated one, which would save you a lot of money on utility bills.

It would also be great if you replaced all your old appliances with new ones that run on more efficient systems that can reduce water and electricity consumption. Eventually, you will find that you not only created a much more sustainable living environment, but you also saved a lot of money because of those practices.

Use Sustainable Resources

The good news is there are always a lot of sustainable resources out there that you can use to make your shipping container home truly sustainable. The catch is, you might need to make a little more effort to find those resources, but the results are definitely worth it. You can start by using eco-friendly insulation. We talked earlier in the book about eco-friendly insulation like cork and wool or cotton, and you have other options like straw and hemp. Depending on your design and the climate in which you are building the shipping container home, it will be much better for the environment if you can use such materials for insulation.

Another resource you might change is your energy source. A solar panel system is ideal for a shipping container home living off the grid. You might pay a few thousand dollars to install the photovoltaic cells, but once that is completed, you will save a lot of money on energy bills in the long run. Solar energy is also one of the eco-friendliest solutions out there to generate electricity.

Recycle

Living in a shipping container home is sustainable in its own way, and if you want to really take things to the next level, consider recycling. This doesn't mean you should give away items to be recycled, you can do it at home. You should obviously have a garden around your shipping container home, and there is no better way to maintain that garden than using compost made out of everyday items we usually dispose of.

So, make a compost bin, in which you can make a compost pile to use in your garden. Things like fruit leftovers, vegetable peels, cotton clothes, tea bags, paper, and a lot more can be used in your compost as a way of recycling these items. When you recycle this much garbage you would usually throw away, it is much better for the environment. Such items would usually get tossed into a landfill, increasing the buildup of methane gas.

Grow Food

Picking up from the last point, and since you will be recycling your garbage, why not grow your own food? You already have a garden, so you absolutely can grow vegetables, and this practice can save a lot of carbon emissions. Plus, making your own food means you control what is added to the soil, so you know there are no added chemicals, and you get to enjoy organic and fresh vegetables.

Build Local

Some people often get dazed by the flash of imported building materials, but if you want to save money and reduce your carbon footprint, the best way to go is using local building materials. While it might always be an available option for everyone, definitely try to find local materials for your shipping container home. Some countries are rich in certain resources, while others might lack the same ones. So, dig a little, and if you find the building materials you need locally, get them. This will significantly lower your carbon footprint, not to mention save you shipping money.

Some people take things a step further and source materials that are not only local, but also surplus. If you look around in your area, you will probably find excess building materials and discarded raw materials that you can use, thus minimizing the need for buying new products. These materials might have some defects, but with a little effort, they can fit into your design and save you a lot of money because they are surplus.

There are many other things you can do for your shipping container home to make sure it is sustainable and poses minimal threat to the environment. From using energy-efficient light bulbs to water-efficient showerheads and toilets, the choice is yours. While these ideas will save you money in the long run, it is helping protect and save the environment that is the ultimate goal.

CONCLUSION

Let's recap the proper order

Your first step will be to find some property. When dealing with the seller of the property or a realtor, ask for the parcel identification number.

Visit your local building or development company (town, city, or county) and verify that that property is zoned as residential. Then double-check to ensure that there are no rules or regulations on the books that would prevent you from putting a mobile home, a modular home, a prefab home, or a shipping container on that parcel of property. Some towns and even counties may have ordinances that restrict the use of shipping containers.

Once you have the property and verified that it's approved for a shipping container or tiny home, now you can start seriously looking for that tiny house or that shipping container or containers depending on your space preferences.

Get it inspected by someone who knows what they're doing. You may be able to spot rust and surface dings, but can you verify whether that's just surface rust or corrosion that you're looking at?

Tip: To verify that any rust you come across is not deep and doesn't extend through the steel into the interior, walk inside and close the door. If you see any light coming through whatsoever, you may be dealing with deep rust or corrosion.

Make sure that the container is square. Most of us have dealt with older homes and even some newer ones that aren't "plumb." This happens when corners aren't square. This can apply to walls, doors and windows. While you might get away with this in a home, in a shipping container, it can cause quite a few problems.

Shipping containers that aren't square and plumb are more prone to developing rust along the seams and corners.

Take the time to properly inspect and clean the container of any possible contaminants. Don't cut corners here. Just like checking an older home to make sure that it has no lead-based paint or asbestos, it's important to also verify as much as possible what that shipping container has transported.

Even if you can't find any information on it, take the steps to properly decontaminate and clean the container prior to working on it. If that means ripping out the old floorboards, do it. Better safe than sorry.

Ready to move in?

Once the basics have been completed, it's time to decorate and move in! This is also an exciting time and doesn't require nearly as much adherence to rules and regs as the other aspects of the conversion process.

However, if you choose to line the walls with paneling, real wood planks, or drywall, you will need to verify if insulation is required. Just because you're on the inside of the house doesn't mean there aren't some rules you'll need to follow.

While adding the finishing touches to your new home, step back and take some pride in what you've accomplished. You're part of a new movement around the globe—to make better use of space, to be less wasteful and to leave a smaller footprint on Mother Earth.

Enjoy the fruits of your labor, and oh, welcome home!

Review the book

Thanks for reading this far. I would be extremely grateful if you would take 1 minute to leave a review on Amazon.

Thank you so much.

REFERENCES

Kempt, Bob. "Importing from China to the UK." Sea and Air Freight Shipping from China to the UK. Barrington Freight, 22 Jan. 2013. Web. 26 Sept. 2016.

"Intermodal Container." Wikipedia. Wikimedia Foundation, n.d. Web. 26 Sept. 2016.

Fernandez, Leo. "How to Build a Shipping Container House." Academia.edu. Nationwide Container Solutions, n.d. Web. 26 Sept. 2016.

Keiren. "27 Extraordinary Shipping Container Homes." Nifty Homestead. Hood Web Management, LLC, 21 Sept. 2016. Web. 26 Sept. 2016.

"Sarah House, an Affordable Green Container Home." Small House Bliss. N.p., 23 Jan. 2014. Web. 26 Sept. 2016.

King, David. "Container Home Review." Container Home Review. N.p., 16 Apr. 2016. Web. 26 Sept. 2016.

"Engineering Modular Buildings from Shipping Containers."Runkleconsulting.com. Runkle Consulting Inc., n.d. Web. 27 Sept. 2016

Manaadiar, Hariesh. "Anatomy of a Shipping Container." Shipping and Freight Resource. Puthan House, 26 Apr. 2014. Web. 26 Sept. 2016.

"Residential Shipping Container Primer (RSCP™)." Residential Shipping Container Primer. RSCP & KOOP.am, LLC, n.d. Web. 26 Sept. 2016

"Residential Foundations: Concrete Slab Vs. Conventional Crawlspace."Donan.com. Donan Engineering Co. Inc., n.d. Web. 27 Sept. 2016.

"Why Do Small Shipping Containers Cost as Much as Big Ones?" CubeDepot. N.p., n.d. Web. 26 Sept. 2016.

Tom. "23 Shipping Container Home Owners Speak Out: "What I Wish I'd Known Before Building My Shipping Container Home"" Container Home Plans. N.p., 14 Apr. 2015. Web. 27 Sept. 2016.

"The Ultimate Guide to Shipping Container Homes - For Sale, Cost, Plans & More." Home Tune Up. N.p., 30 June 2014. Web. 26 Sept. 2016.

Becker, Joshua. "12 Reasons Why You'll Be Happier in a Smaller Home. "Becoming Minimalist. Joshua Becker, 29 May 2014. Web. 26 Sept. 2016.

www.ingramcontent.com/pod-product-compliance
Lightning Source LLC
LaVergne TN
LVHW051057100526
838202LV00086BA/6467